INTERCESSIONS
FOR THE CHRISTIAN PEOPLE

INTERCESSIONS
FOR
THE CHRISTIAN PEOPLE

Prayers of the People for Cycles A, B, and C
of the
Roman, Episcopal, and Lutheran
Lectionaries

Edited by Gail Ramshaw

PUEBLO PUBLISHING COMPANY

New York

Design: Frank Kacmarcik

Writers:

J. Neil Alexander, Herbert Brokering, Edgar S. Brown, Jr., Brian Burchfield, Patrick Byrne, Andrew D. Ciferni O Praem, Madeleine Sophie Cooney RSCJ, Cheryl E. Dieter, James Empereur, Richard N. Fragomeni, Jann Esther Boyd Fullenwieder, The Rt. Rev. Frank T. Griswold, John Gallen SJ, Gabe Huck, Kathleen Hughes RSCJ, Sharon Karam RSCJ, Aelred Kavanagh OSB, Gordon Lathrop, Carol Luebering, Anne C. McGuire, Paul Marshall, Peter Mazar, John Allyn Melloh SM, Leonel L. Mitchell, Gilbert Ostdiek OFM, Constance Parvey, Phillip H. Pfatteicher, David N. Power OMI, Frank C. Quinn OP, Gail Ramshaw, Don E. Saliers, Peter J. Scagnelli, Barbara Schmich, Mark Searle, R. Kevin Seasoltz OSB, Frank C. Senn, Joseph A. Serano O Praem, Mary Ann Simcoe, Virginia Sloyan, Ralph F. Smith, S. Anita Stauffer, Daniel Stevick, Columba Stewart OSB, Francis Patrick Sullivan, Samuel Torvend OP, Ralph R. Van Loon, Elizabeth-Anne Vanek, Louis Weil, James A. Wilde, Donald Wisner

ISBN 0-916134-91-1

Printed in the United States of America

TABLE OF CONTENTS

INTRODUCTION

"Then we all stand up together and offer prayers."
Justin, 150 CE

With this volume Pueblo Publishing Company presents a collection of prayers of the people. Responding to the continual need of Christian assemblies to craft each week a set of intercessory prayers, we have commissioned this collection of prayers of the faithful from over fifty Roman Catholic, Episcopalian, and Lutheran writers throughout the land.

These intercessory prayers are based on the three-year Roman Catholic, Episcopal, and Lutheran lectionaries. For nearly all the Sundays and major holy days, there is enough congruence, even granting some diversity in lessons, that a single intercessory prayer for the three communions is quite possible. Each prayer is titled with the Roman Catholic, Episcopalian, and Lutheran names of the appropriate Sunday or festival. The table of contents will guide you to the appropriate page for each prayer.

These prayers were written for the imaginary "average" Sunday assembly. It is strongly encouraged that each assembly of worshipers adapt these model prayers to its specific situation. These prayers are only the skeletons which you must flesh out, adding intercessions, including names and concerns, keeping silence, or substituting other congregational responses, thus rendering these model prayers appropriate to your assembly. Due to the great diversity of Christian assemblies and the number of years these prayers might be prayed, the printed texts are more generalized than prayers of intercession should be. For example, prayers for the poor will be crafted differently, depending on the economic level of a specific assembly. This publication calls you to specificity: and if "the incurable disease" concerning your community at this time is AIDS, do not hesitate to cry out its name before God.

The prayers have been guided by the historic pattern of prayers of the faithful: a brief introduction inviting the assembly to prayer; five or six petitions, including prayers for the church, the world, those in need, and the local community; opportunity for petitions specific to the assembly; and a concluding prayer. Some of the prayers are cast as bids, calling the people to prayer; others are cast as petitions, addressed to God. In both cases, the prayers include a line of congregational response which is indicated at the end of the invitation to prayer. The prayers are informed by the content and imagery of the day and the season, and vary in style and tone, depending on their author.

Historically, it was the task of the deacon or assisting minister to offer the intercessory prayer. It is hoped that these prayers will be amended and offered by someone other than the presider of the eucharist. The reader ought to pray these prayers vigorously, rather than reading them pedantically, and caught up in the spirit of corporate prayer the people can follow along without a printed text. The responses are designed to encourage the people's lively participation.

The ecumenical nature of this collection is its hidden gift. By this collection of intercessory prayers, Christians throughout North America who hear the lessons in Roman Catholic, Episcopalian, and Lutheran churches are helping one another pray. Although the churches do not yet share the bread and wine together, we hear the same lessons and can pray in common. As "we all stand up together and offer prayers," may our constant prayer be for the unity of the all Christians.

Gail Ramshaw, editor

FOR ANY DAY

In peace, let us pray to the Lord, saying: Lord, have mercy.

For the church and its bishops, for the newly baptized, and for all the faithful, let us pray to the Lord.

For the nations, for all rulers, legislators, and judges, and for an increase of justice in our lands, let us pray to the Lord.

For the United Nations, and for all who work for peace, let us pray to the Lord.

For our community, and for solace and security for all its people, let us pray to the Lord.

For this assembly, and for our growth in grace, let us pray to the Lord.

For good weather, and for all who work to preserve God's creation, let us pray to the Lord.

For rich harvests, and for an equitable distribution of food throughout the world, let us pray to the Lord.

For all in any need, for the hungry and the homeless, for victims of war and injustice, and for prisoners, let us pray to the Lord.

For all who suffer, for the sick and infirm [especially N.], for all with incurable illness, and for all who this day will die, let us pray to the Lord.

[Here other intercessions may be offered.]

For all who have died in the faith of Christ [especially N.,] and for the promise of resurrection to be fulfilled, let us pray to the Lord.

Into your mercy we commend ourselves, and for peace at the last we pray, that all your creation may give you praise and worship, through your Son, Jesus Christ our Lord.

SUNDAYS, MAJOR HOLY DAYS, AND SOLEMNITIES,

CYCLE A

FIRST SUNDAY OF ADVENT A

God calls us to love one another. As a sign of that love, let us lift up our prayer to God for the needs of all people throughout the world, saying: O God, in your mercy, hear our prayer.

We pray for the peace of the world, that our instruments of war may be transformed into instruments of peace, and that nations shall cease to learn war any more. O God, in your mercy,

We pray for the church, that we may become more and more a means of grace and peace in the world. O God, in your mercy,

We pray for all people of good will who seek to cast off the works of darkness, that we may be enlightened through our service of others in the name of Christ. O God, in your mercy,

We pray for all who are in need [especially N.], that we may be alert to the presence of Christ in them and ready to reach out in love. O God, in your mercy,

We pray for those who are assembled here today, that we may be clothed with the Lord Jesus Christ and go forth from this place to be Christ in the world. O God, in your mercy,

We pray for all who have asked for our prayers [especially N.], that we may faithfully wait upon God with confidence in that love which sustains us in every moment of our lives. O God, in your mercy,

[Here other intercessions may be offered.]

We praise you, Lord our God, that you have called us to be your people and the instruments of your presence in the world. Grant us grace to discern your will and the strength to do it, through Christ our Lord.

SECOND SUNDAY OF ADVENT A

The prophet John the Baptist preached a repentance which would bear fruit in the lives of those who heard him. In penitence and faith, let us offer to God our prayer for all people, saying: In the name of Christ, hear our prayer.

We pray for the church throughout the world, [remembering especially our sisters and brothers in N.,] and for all those ordained to particular ministries for the building up for the body of Christ [especially N.],that in our diverse vocations we may serve to the glory of God. In the name of Christ,

We pray for this nation and for all the nations of the world, remembering especially those who are victims of political or social injustice. We pray for those whom we have elected to public office [especially N.], and for political leaders everywhere, that they may administer the tasks of government with courage and equity. In the name of Christ,

We pray for the sick, the elderly, and those who live alone [especially N.]. We pray for those who are overworked and for those who cannot find work. Send upon them the power of the Holy Spirit, that they may abound in hope. In the name of Christ,

We pray for this community, for our neighbors and friends, for those with whom we study and work. Guide and strengthen us all in our common life that we may know the gifts of your grace and love. In the name of Christ,

[Here other intercessions may be offered.]

We offer these prayers to you, our God, in penitence for what is past and in faith that your work in us will bear fruit as we seek to do your will, for you alone are the Holy One. May our lives give honor to you, through Christ our Lord.

THIRD SUNDAY OF ADVENT A

Jesus said that the signs of God's dominion were to be seen in the healing of the sick, the raising of the dead to new life, and the preaching of good news to the poor. Let us pray that our lives may be the instruments of God's work in the world, saying: O God, most worthy of praise, hear our prayer.

We thank you, God, for the gift of creation. Grant that we who bear your image may be faithful stewards of your gift and administer its bounty with wisdom for the good of all your creatures. O God, most worthy of praise,

We thank you that you have called us to be your people. Give us patience as we await your coming, and grant us wisdom to discern your will in our daily lives, that each of us may serve others for the building up of our common life. O God, most worthy of praise,

We thank you for the community of faith throughout the world. Strengthen your church as it witnesses to your love [and hear our prayers for N.]. Guide us in the fulfillment of your mission, that all may be one. O God, most worthy of praise,

We thank you for the privilege of ministering to others. We remember before you all who are sick or in need [especially N.]. We pray for those who have died [especially N.]. Grant us the grace to accept suffering with patience and to be strengthened by our common life in the body of Christ. O God, most worthy of praise,

We thank you for your countless gifts. [We praise you for . . . .] Above all, we thank you for the coming of our Savior Jesus Christ, and for our unity in him through baptism. O God, most worthy of praise,

[Here other intercessions may be offered.]

We offer our thanksgiving and prayers to you, the one God and the source of light and life, now and forever

FOURTH SUNDAY OF ADVENT A

Mary, the mother of Christ, is a sign to the church of faithful obedience to the will of God. As we come to the commemoration of the birth of Christ, let us pray that we, like Mary, hear God's word and respond in obedient faith to the coming of Christ, saying: O God, who is with us, hear our prayer.

Let us pray for the church, that every baptized member may manifest Christ in the world. O God, who is with us,

Let us pray for the leaders of government in every nation [especially N.], that they may have wisdom to choose what serves the common good. O God, who is with us,

Let us pray for all who are in need, remembering all who are sick, the elderly, those who are alone, and all who minister to them, [especially N.,] that we all may be strengthened by the presence of Christ as the sign of God's love. O God, who is with us,

Let us pray for those with whom we share our daily lives, our families, friends and neighbors, and those with whom we work and play, that we may all be strengthened and sustained by God's presence with us. O God, who is with us,

[Here other intercessions may be offered.]

Let us pray for those who have died [especially N.], that they may rest in peace. May we wait in hope for the promise of resurrection with them. O God, who is with us,

Hasten, O God, the coming of your dominion. Come to us in Christ, that we who live by faith in this world may see our faith confirmed in the world to come, through our risen Christ.

CHRISTMAS MASS AT MIDNIGHT A
CHRISTMAS DAY I A
THE NATIVITY OF OUR LORD 1 A

*My sisters and brothers in the peace of God, all the gifts we shall give
and receive in these days are but small tokens of the gift that shines
forth in God's word made flesh this night. From grateful hearts let us
intercede for all who find themselves longing for this deepest, truest
gift, saying: Lord, hear our prayer.*

That the peace proclaimed by angels in the shepherds' field
might be realized on every field of war and on every street of
violence, let us pray to the Lord.

That the child born to us might find in our hearts warm welcome by our openness to the needs of the homeless and the
hungry, let us pray to the Lord.

That in this time of gift-giving we might become more respon-
sive to the abandoned, the despairing, and the mourning, let
us pray to the Lord.

That the rejoicing of this day might be a bond leading us to true
communion of life and worship, let us pray to the Lord.

That the joy and consolation of the Wonderful Counselor might
enliven all who are struck down by disease and illness [espe-
cially N.], let us pray to the Lord.

[Here other intercessions may be offered.]

That the blessed hope we celebrate this night might be the
fulfillment of all who have gone before us in faith [especially
N.], let us pray to the Lord.

*God of darkness and silence, you have pierced the quiet of this night by
the utterance of your word in our flesh. May our words of praise and
petition be strong echoes of your Christmas word, so that all might
come to the peace you promise in Jesus, who is Lord and God this
night and forever.*

CHRISTMAS MASS DURING THE DAY A
CHRISTMAS DAY III A
THE NATIVITY OF OUR LORD 2 A

Dear sisters and brothers, God has pitched a tent in our midst. God's word has taken our flesh. That all may know God's presence bringing us together, it is fitting that our flesh should call to God in holy words of petition, saying: Lord, have mercy.

That the feet of each of us might be made beautiful through our proclamation of peace at table, desk, and lathe, as well as in every place where violence threatens, let us pray to the Lord.

That the word which conquers darkness might enlighten the blindness which keeps Christ's followers separated and at odds, let us pray to the Lord.

That our celebration of God's first-born might inspire and quicken in us protection and nurture of all human life, and especially the children, let us pray to the Lord.

That God's dwelling among us might lead us to shelter the homeless, feed the hungry, and support those who minister to them, let us pray to the Lord.

That the power of the word might fill our hearts and minds, so that the gospel be preached with greater courage and strength to the ends of the earth, let us pray to the Lord.

That the love of God following upon love might work for the healing of the sick [especially N.], let us pray to the Lord.

[Here other intercessions may be offered.]

O God, the source of light and sound, your word dispels our darkness, and your light speaks to our hearts. As we praise you, we beg that your power overwhelm us, that all the world might find us the more perfect ministers of your presence. Thus may you be glorified this Christmas Day and forever in Christ Jesus our Lord.

HOLY FAMILY A
FIRST SUNDAY AFTER CHRISTMAS A

God has clothed all things with mercy and prepared the earth as for a wedding by taking on our flesh in Christ. Trusting in that mercy, let our prayers join the festival, saying: O God, mighty God, merciful God, hear our prayer.

For the churches, that this assembly and all assemblies may be cradles for the word of Christ, filled with harmony and witnessing with thanksgiving, O God, mighty God, merciful God,

For the bishops and all the leaders of the church, that in word and deed they may show forth the love and pity with which you clothe creation and all its peoples, O God, mighty God, merciful God,

For refugees and for those who experience a pitiless world [especially N.], that you may bring them to places of safety they may call home, O God, mighty God, merciful God,

For all families, that their common life may be marked by mutual honor, respect, and forgiveness, and that homes may become places of hospitality to the stranger, O God, mighty God, merciful God,

For the victims of family violence, that you quickly bring relief, justice, and healing, O God, mighty God, merciful God,

For the earth which you honored in the incarnation of your Son, and for us creatures, that a spirit of joy in its goodness and care for its future may be poured out upon us all, O God, mighty God, merciful God,

[Here other intercessions may be offered.]

Rejoicing with all the saints, with Mary and Joseph, with Stephen, John, and all the Holy Innocents, we commend these prayers and all our life to you, O God, through Jesus Christ our Lord.

SECOND SUNDAY AFTER CHRISTMAS A

Rejoicing in the mercy of God, manifested for our salvation in the birth of Jesus Christ our Savior, let us pray for all the needs of the world, saying: Lord, have mercy.

That the churches may know God and God's wisdom, that they may be assemblies of God's grace, let us pray to the Lord.

That the leaders of the church [especially N.], along with all preachers and ministers, bishops and teachers, may be formed by that wisdom of God manifest in Israel and born among us in Jesus Christ, let us pray to the Lord.

That the leaders of nations may be brought to your wisdom, may honor peace, and may protect the earth's resources, let us pray to the Lord.

That the Jewish people may know continual comfort in God's mercy and great joy in the wisdom of their heritage, let us pray to the Lord.

That those who suffer the ravages of winter, the hungry, the elderly, the unemployed, and the sick among us [especially N.] may be clothed with healing and comfort, let us pray to the Lord.

That this assembly may be refreshed in its mission to bear witness to the word and wisdom of God, let us pray to the Lord.

[Here other intercessions may be offered.]

Into your hands, merciful God, we commend all for whom we pray, through Jesus Christ our Lord.

THE EPIPHANY OF OUR LORD A

God's glory has been veiled in flesh. Our flesh has become a glorious epiphany. Let us then present before the Lord of glory our gift of prayer for those who are in need, saying: Lord, hear our prayer.

For all who walk in the darkness of violence and oppression, and for all who by their life and preaching cast into that darkness the light of God's peace and justice, let us pray to the Lord.

For all who carry on the teaching of prophets and apostles, and for the full communion in life and worship of those who receive God's word, let us pray to the Lord.

For all who have at their disposal this world's riches, and for all who call out to them, let us pray to the Lord.

For all who raise their eyes to the heavens looking for healing and deliverance [especially N.], let us pray to the Lord.

For the rulers of the earth, and for every child that stands in need of their protection, let us pray to the Lord.

[Here other intercessions may be offered.]

For all who through death have passed into the full epiphany of God's glory [especially N.], let us pray to the Lord.

O God of stars and journeys, you lead us day by day to the joyful vision of your light. Move us by the power of your word that we too might open our gifts for others and so receive in our hearts the child of Bethlehem. So may you be praised and adored through the same Christ our Lord, in the Holy Spirit, this day of your Epiphany, now and forever.

BAPTISM OF OUR LORD A
FIRST SUNDAY AFTER EPIPHANY A

Through our baptism we are joined to Christ as God's beloved children. As sisters and brothers in the Spirit, let us call to God for the needs of the world and the church, saying: Lord, have mercy.

For the victory of justice among the nations, and for the outpouring of the Spirit's gift of peace, let us pray to the Lord.

For the liberation of all oppressed and imprisoned, for the preaching of the liberating gospel, and for reconciliation of all who oppress and persecute others, let us pray to the Lord.

For the healing of all who are gripped by despair and frustration, and for all who inspire them with hope and joy, let us pray to the Lord.

For all in this community to be alive to the call of their baptism, for the newly baptized [especially N.], and for all who guide and teach along the way, let us pray to the Lord.

For all who in their illness look to us for strength and healing in Christ [especially N.], let us pray to the Lord.

[Here other intercessions may be offered.]

For all who have died in the expectation of Christ's full victory in their life and death [especially N.], let us pray to the Lord.

Loving God and Father of our Lord Jesus Christ, as your favor comes upon us, enlighten us to see those who search for the victory of your love. Make of us your gracious servants, that the world may rest in your peace and sing your praises with full hearts and voices, through the same Jesus Christ, your Son and our Lord, who with you and the Holy Spirit is one God, this day and forever.

SECOND SUNDAY IN ORDINARY TIME A
SECOND SUNDAY AFTER EPIPHANY A

Let us pray for the church and for the world, that all people may shine with the radiance of Christ, saying: Lord, hear our prayer.

For the church of God, that all who in every place call on the name of our Lord Jesus Christ may be filled with all spiritual gifts and preserved in faith and peace, let us pray to the Lord.

For the mission of the church, that like the disciples we may bring our brothers and sisters everywhere to come and see the Savior, let us pray to the Lord.

For the peoples of the world, and all who govern them, and for peace and mutual respect among nations, let us pray to the Lord.

For those impoverished, oppressed, or humiliated by our way of life, that justice, equality, and reconciliation may unite all of God's creation, let us pray to the Lord.

For those who are sick, for those who mourn, and for those in any kind of trouble [especially N.], that our actions may show God's care for them, let us pray to the Lord.

[Here other intercessions may be offered.]

For all who have died in the peace of Christ, [especially N.] and for all the departed, let us pray to the Lord.

Eternal God, hear the prayers of all your people, and give us the will and the courage to serve you throughout the world, until the day of our Lord Jesus Christ, in whose name we pray.

THIRD SUNDAY IN ORDINARY TIME A
THIRD SUNDAY AFTER EPIPHANY A

Let us pray for the church and the world, saying: Lord, have mercy.

Holy God, we pray for all your people, baptized in the name of Christ. Heal our divisions, and give us one mind in Christ. For this we pray to you, O Lord:

Stir up your church to make the power of the cross known to all, that people everywhere may see your great light. For this we pray to you, O Lord:

Lift from all people the burdens of poverty, war and injustice. Break every rod of oppression throughout the earth. For this we pray to you, O Lord:

Guide those who make and execute our laws, and those who maintain our safety, that all people may know their worth as your creation. For this we pray to you, O Lord:

Strengthen us to care for the poor, the imprisoned, and all who suffer. Open our hands and our hearts to embrace all who are in need [especially N.]. For this we pray to you, O Lord:

[Here other intercessions may be offered.]

We remember before you [N. and] all whom we love but see no more. Give them eternal rest. For this we pray to you, O Lord:

O God, you revealed your will to prophets and sages. By your Holy Spirit, show us how to serve you today, that all nations may know you in our love, through Christ our Lord.

FOURTH SUNDAY IN ORDINARY TIME A
FOURTH SUNDAY AFTER EPIPHANY A

For the church and for all your creation, we pray to you, Lord God,
saying: Lord, hear our prayer.

Blessed are the poor in spirit; theirs is the dominion of heaven.
And so we pray: Unite the church, guide [N. and] all its leaders; let us show the world the love of Jesus.

Blessed are the pure in heart; they shall see God. And so we
pray: Give your people the will and the courage to value your
service above all lesser goods.

Blessed are the peacemakers, God's own children. And so we
pray: Bring peace to the world, security to the nations, and
safety to the cities.

Blessed are those who hunger and thirst for righteousness, for
they shall be satisfied. And so we pray: Remove from us prejudice and injustice, and raise up among us those who will labor
for the good of all whom you have made.

Blessed are the merciful, for they shall obtain mercy. And so
we pray: Be present with those who are sick, imprisoned, or in
distress [especially N.]; make us quick to love and serve our
neighbors.

[Here other intercessions may be offered.]

Rejoice and be glad, their reward is great in heaven. And so we
pray: We remember all who have witnessed to your love with
their lives; give us strength to testify to Christ before the rulers
of our own day.

Almighty God, you have taught us to do justice, love kindness, and
practice humility before you; make our faith active in love, that your
name may be praised and your people served throughout the earth,
through Christ our Lord.

FIFTH SUNDAY IN ORDINARY TIME A
FIFTH SUNDAY AFTER EPIPHANY A

Let us pray for all people, for all nations, and for the church, offering silent prayer as we are bidden.

I ask your prayers for God's church, for [N. and] all who serve it, for this assembly, and for all God's people everywhere. Pray for the church.

I ask your prayers for the good earth, that all people may respect its resources, preserve its future, and enjoy its fruits in their season. Pray for the soil and the sea.

I ask your prayers for the leaders of the nations, that they may act deliberately and dispassionately, and for the good of all. Pray for those who govern.

I ask your prayers for peace, that the peoples of the world may live in safety and without fear. Pray for peace.

I ask your prayers for the wealthy, the free, and the healthy, that they may use their possessions to aid those in need. Pray for compassion among people.

I ask your prayers for the sick, the sorrowing, and those who are alone [especially N.]. Pray for those in any need or trouble.

[Here other intercessions may be offered.]

I ask your prayers for the faithful departed [especially N.], that God give them eternal rest. Pray for those who have died.

God of all the living, hear the prayers of your faithful people, and grant our requests. Strengthen us for the tasks you give us, and bring us at last to praise you forever with your saints, through Christ our Lord.

SIXTH SUNDAY IN ORDINARY TIME A
SIXTH SUNDAY AFTER EPIPHANY A
PROPER 1 A

Our gracious God calls us to be ministers of reconciliation in a world refusing honor to God. In acknowledgement of our Lord's command, let us place our prayers before God saying: Lord, hear our prayer.

For the courage to live out God's commandments, graciously and without reservation, let us pray to the Lord.

For zealous preachers of the word [especially N.], that by the Holy Spirit, they open the ears of their hearers to the good news of salvation and their eyes to the loveliness of God's wisdom, let us pray to the Lord.

For those chosen to govern peoples and nations, that God grant them the wisdom to promote the welfare of their people and the courage to work towards true peace, let us pray to the Lord.

For those who suffer from any form of oppression, that their tormentors learn to fear God's will and follow God's love, let us pray to the Lord.

For all who are sick and in need of our prayers [especially N.], that through our loving concern that they be comforted in their distress, let us pray to the Lord.

For our own needs, and that we may rejoice in Christ's command to celebrate his redeeming death and resurrection and so live out the mystery of the cross in our daily lives, let us pray to the Lord.

[Here other intercessions may be offered.]

For those who have yearned to see God face to face [especially N.], that they may receive eternal rest, let us pray to the Lord.

Loving God, in your unsearchable wisdom you command us to do what is right and good, so that through faith-filled action we may come to recognize your loving concern for us. May we always be single-minded in carrying out your commands, especially to be reconciled with one another, and to approach your holy table in peace and unity. We make this prayer through Christ our Lord.

SEVENTH SUNDAY IN ORDINARY TIME A
SEVENTH SUNDAY AFTER EPIPHANY A
PROPER 2 A

The all-wise and loving God calls us to be fools for the sake of Christ. Although we cannot accomplish what is right and good, may our prayers please our God and bring our Lord's response, as we say: Lord, have mercy.

For Christians throughout the world, that their loving concern may extend to all God's people, and that they may never by word or deed show contempt for their neighbor, we pray:

For Christian leaders, that their imitation of God's holiness may bear fruit in words of compassion and works of loving-kindness, we pray:

For civic leaders, that in obedience to God's commands they may promote the welfare of all their citizens, we pray:

For all who suffer in any way [especially N.], that they may not despair of joining their sufferings to those of Christ, we pray:

For our Jewish sisters and brothers, that they may be faithful to God's call to holiness, we pray:

For the needs of this assembly, that our sharing of God's holy gifts around this table may bear fruit in our daily lives, we pray:

[Here other intercessions may be offered.]

For our brothers and sisters who have died [especially N.], that having built up the church by their lives of holiness, they may now reside in the heavenly Jerusalem, chanting the glory of God, we pray:

All holy God, your wisdom illuminates our folly, and your love shows forth the shallowness of our concern. By the prayer we offer may we receive the grace to avoid all vengeance and hatred and the courage to live out our Christian convictions. We make this prayer in the name of Christ our Lord.

EIGHTH SUNDAY IN ORDINARY TIME A
EIGHTH SUNDAY AFTER EPIPHANY A
PROPER 3 A

Our all-powerful God calls us to be stewards of the mysteries of God's dominion. That we may enjoy the blessings God has promised, let us offer to God our prayers, saying: Lord, hear our prayer.

For all Christians, that they not fear to be despised for the love of Christ and for adherence to God's commands, let us pray to the Lord.

For those who minister to the people of God, that they will be faithful guardians of all that God has revealed and willing servants to their people, let us pray to the Lord.

For elected officials [especially N.], that they work for the good of their people, let us pray to the Lord.

For those who suffer in any way, especially the innocent [and N.], that they may experience the tender care of God, let us pray to the Lord.

For the courage to accept the challenges of the day, not avoiding them for the illusory promises of tomorrow, let us pray to the Lord.

For our own needs, that the bread we share and the wine we drink may strengthen us to build up the body of Christ, so that one day from east to west and north to south all God's people will converge on the city of God, the heavenly Jerusalem, let us pray to the Lord.

[Here other intercessions may be offered.]

For those who have died [especially N.], that in passing beyond the cares of this world they may no longer be in want for any good thing, let us pray to the Lord.

God of majesty, you have called us to serve you alone. Hear our prayers, and enable us to avoid worry about our own needs, that we may always be sensitive to the needs of others. We make this prayer through Christ our Lord.

LAST SUNDAY AFTER EPIPHANY A
TRANSFIGURATION OF OUR LORD A

Let us pray to God who commanded the light to shine out of darkness and whose glory is like a devouring fire, saying: Lord, in your mercy, hear our prayer.

That the church may be continually uplifted by the vision of the king in all his beauty, be rescued from all fear, and in confidence face the future: Lord, in your mercy,

That the church may be conformed to Christ the Son of God, share his sufferings, become like him in his death, and know the power of his resurrection: Lord, in your mercy,

That your people may hear the prophets' testimony, see you clearly in the records of those who were eyewitnesses of your majesty, and do your will, preparing for your glorious coming on the Last Day: Lord, in your mercy,

That the nations of the earth may more and more perfect the rule of law and administer justice after the example of Moses, the lawgiver and judge of your people: Lord, in your mercy,

That the church may heed the call of God in Christ Jesus to descend from the heights of vision and to serve those who are needy, desolate, and forgotten: Lord, in your mercy,

That the suffering, the lonely, the disconsolate, the dying, and those who mourn [especially N.] may know the transforming light of your presence: Lord, in your mercy,

That the whole church may persevere in the proclamation of the gospel until the day dawns and Christ, the morning star who knows no setting, arises, that all the world may walk in his light: Lord, in your mercy,

[Here other intercessions may be offered.]

Arise, O Morning Star, and in your rising lift us to behold with all the saints the majestic glory of God, so that through the shadows and darkness of this world we may ever press toward the glory of the world to come, where with the Father and the Holy Spirit you live and reign , God forever.

ASH WEDNESDAY A

Our compassionate and yet all-powerful God has called us to repentance. May our prayers and our fasting assist us in coming before God with pure hearts and minds. Today is the acceptable time; let us pray, saying: Lord, have mercy.

For all Christians, that embracing their lenten discipline with joy, the cross of Christ may be their banner and the pledge of resurrection their hope, we pray:

For those preparing for baptism, that their observance of the lenten season strengthen their resolve to receive God's gift of new life, we pray:

For our young people, that they find Lent a time of profound renewal and Easter a season of unsurpassing joy, we pray:

For all churches, that Lent be a time of repentance for sins against unity of the body of Christ, we pray:

For our parish concerns [especially . . .], that we remember the needs of others as we purify our own hearts and minds, we pray:

For this assembly, that as we celebrate our union with Christ in this holy meal we may not grow weary of proclaiming his saving death and resurrection to the whole world, we pray:

For those who suffer from illness, especially the elderly [and N.], that they may receive the consolation of knowing the love of their crucified Savior, we pray:

[Here other intercessions may be offered.]

O God, as you called the Israelites to repent of their sins, so now you call us to fasting and prayer, in repentance for wandering from you. Never let us lose our way, and guide us during our lenten journey that we arrive at the Easter Vigil, ready once more to celebrate our passage with Christ from death to life, from despair to hope, trusting in the life of Christ, our Lord.

FIRST SUNDAY IN LENT A

Our great God has formed the dust of our being in the midst of the waters of creation. Let us adore the Righteous One, saying: O God, feed us with mercy: Lord, hear our prayer.

For the Tree of Golgotha, our true tree of life, by whose just fruit we live, the church worships you, O God. May your people ever praise and serve you and all the world's people. O God, feed us with mercy:

O God of the seas and rains, we praise you for watering and sustaining all things living. We bless you for the waters flowing from Jesus' pierced side. Give to all candidates of baptism, and to all the baptized, the sure hope of your grace. O God, feed us with mercy:

Send us to the nations where there is a famine of the word; show us those who await the bread of life; and confront us with those who suffer in hunger. May our abundance supply their need. O God, feed us with mercy:

Lord and judge of all, confirm what is good and just in the hearts of those who rule the nations. Make all in authority to govern in justice the peoples whom you have made. O God, feed us with mercy:

For all who desire wisdom, for all who need hands to bear them up, for the naked and the outcast, for the sick and the dying [especially N.], for all in need of your gift of abundant health, we pray for your mercy:

[Here other intercessions may be offered.]

For all the holy people before us who served you as their only wisdom amid life's temptations [especially N.], we give you thanks, O God. Give your holy angels charge over us, and bring us who live in the wilderness of time from the waters of baptism into the garden of your great love, where we will be no longer in hunger, but filled with your life forever, through Christ our Lord.

SECOND SUNDAY IN LENT A

Let us come before God in this Lententide, praising and blessing and adoring our everliving God, saying: In your glorious mercy, Lord, hear our prayer.

O God, who spoke through the prophets and who lives in the only begotten one, show to your church all things. Make us hear your purpose and receive your grace; confirm in your truth all the baptized, especially bishops and clergy, theologians and teachers, mystics and martyrs. In your glorious mercy:

Lord of promise and deliverance, we thank you for birthing us in the waters of baptism and for drowning our death in your unending life. We beg that your love well up within us, that our whole lives may worship you. In your glorious mercy:

God of the people of Israel, Sovereign of every nation, grant your vision of mercy and justice to all who rule in the earth [especially N.]. Prosper the labors of those seeking peace. Assist all who work for reconciliation in the streets and for reformation in prisons. In your glorious mercy:

O Holy One with the pierced limbs and side, bind us to all whose who suffer. Keep us mindful of all innocent victims, all the oppressed, all the dying. Reveal to us those who are despised, the outcast, the alien, the forlorn. Look upon the sick [especially N.]. Summon us to restlessness until all who suffer find rest from their sorrow. In your glorious mercy:

[Here other intercessions may be offered.]

God of Abraham and Sarah, the great I AM, we give you thanks for the signs of your radiant presence in the faith of our forebears [especially N.]. Bless us with awe to receive their testimony. Transfigure us by the gift of faith for our life's journey, until we behold face to face your glorious beauty, through Christ our Lord.

We have been birthed for holiness in Christ, by whose arduous labor we are awakened to life. That the wounds of our crucified Christ may not be in vain, let us pray to the Lord, saying: We beg for mercy, O God.

For the whole church catholic, for an end to our divisions, for all who lead and all who minister, and for all the baptized, we pray:

For all who seek the living waters of baptism, and for all sponsors, we pray:

For the nations, for peacemakers, for all the world's peoples, for the governing authorities in every city and state [especially N.], and for the wealthy and free to uplift the poor and oppressed, we pray:

For the will to give all your people access to your grace, and for the will to supply food and sustenance to all the world's people, we pray:

For all whom we avoid, those we consider ungodly, the outcasts and beggars, the downtrodden, for our enemies, and for an end to our hardness of heart, we pray:

For all who yearn for health, for the handicapped, for those in mental anguish or spiritual turmoil, for the incurably ill, and for all who remember and care for them, [especially N.], we pray:

For hearts to do what is good and right and true, and for humility before Christ, that we may never murmur against you, O holy God, we pray:

[Here other intercessions may be offered.]

We praise you, God of our hope, for all the faithful before us who entered into your labors and worshiped you in truth [especially N.]. That we may live faithful to eternal life, we pray:

Pour your love into our hearts, O God of peace. Give us joy in our suffering, endurance in trials, character in times of weakness, and hope in adversity. So may we live, birthed always anew in you, who has gasped and panted for our life, now and forever.

FOURTH SUNDAY IN LENT A

God has consecrated us in baptism's gracious waters to be a holy people. That we may be ever anointed with gladness, let us turn to our God in prayer, saying: God of all gladness, have mercy upon us.

We pray for the church, for an end to division and indignation, for all the people washed and sent by Christ, and for a renewal of God's fulfilling Spirit: God of all gladness,

We pray for all who beg for life, for all baptismal candidates awaiting the pool of grace, and for hearts of devout faith: God of all gladness,

We pray for all who are called to govern in justice and peace, for an end to all works of darkness, for all the peoples created in God's image, and for a Spirit of wisdom and mercy to rule the mighty: God of all gladness,

We pray for all condemned to die, for all victims of illegal arrest and oppression, for all who are tortured, for their families, and for all who work for liberation: God of all gladness,

We pray for the forgotten and abandoned, for all who are in anguish, for the guilt-ridden, for all in need of the Spirit, for the sick, the grieving, and the dying [especially N.], that they may be uplifted: God of all gladness,

For all brothers and sisters, mothers and fathers, spouses and families, friends and companions, that there may be love and mutual reverence: God of all gladness,

[Here other intercessions may be offered.]

We praise you, God of our hope, for all the children of light who have gone before us and now stand in your radiant countenance [especially N.]. Give us the light of Christ, that we may leap up in our darkness and rise from death at the last, into the life of gladness in Christ our Lord.

FIFTH SUNDAY IN LENT A

In our baptism we have been called to rise from the dead and to live with Christ in the Spirit of God. Bonded to the whole people of God in baptism, let us pray for the church and for all people in their need, saying: Lord, in your mercy, hear our prayer.

For the unity of the scattered people of God: Lord, in your mercy,

For all who lead the church, and for all the baptized in their lenten pilgrimage: Lord, in your mercy,

For those who are preparing for baptismal death and resurrection: Lord, in your mercy,

For the leaders of nations, and for peace throughout the world: Lord, in your mercy,

For all who suffer, for all the dying, for those who grieve [especially N.]: Lord, in your mercy,

For those whose burden is too deep for words: Lord, in your mercy,

[Here other intercessions may be offered.]

In thanksgiving for the saints and martyrs, and for all who are heirs of Christ's suffering and glory: Lord, in your mercy,

O God, in the waters of baptism you rescue our lives from death and make us your children. Into your hands we commend ourselves and all for whom we pray, through your Son, Jesus Christ our Lord.

SUNDAY OF THE PASSION A
PALM SUNDAY A

On this day the church hears again the passion of our Lord, into which we are baptized. Recreated by the mind of Christ, let us pray for the whole people of God in Christ Jesus, and for all people according to their needs, saying: Lord, have mercy.

For the whole church throughout the world, its bishops, clergy, and all the baptized, let us pray to the Lord.

For those who are preparing for baptism, and for their teachers and sponsors, let us pray to the Lord.

For peace among nations and forbearance among all people, let us pray to the Lord.

For this assembly as we walk the road toward the cross, let us pray to the Lord.

For the weary and the sick, and for those who are consumed with sorrow [especially N.], let us pray to the Lord.

[Here other intercessions may be offered.]

We give thanks for all the departed who had the mind of Christ and were humble servants of God. For ourselves, that we may be obedient even unto death, let us pray to the Lord.

Into your hands, O God, we commend ourselves and all for whom we pray, through your Son, Jesus Christ our Lord.

HOLY THURSDAY A
MAUNDY THURSDAY A

On this holy day we dine together as the body of Christ, and at the table come to love and serve one another. On this holy day, then, let us pray for the church and the world, saying: Lord, in your mercy, hear our prayer.

For the whole church of God, that it may grow in unity and servanthood: Lord, in your mercy,

For our congregation, that in these holy days we may grow in love for one another and for all people: Lord, in your mercy,

For those who will be baptized at Easter, that they may rejoice in their passage through death into new life: Lord, in your mercy,

For all the leaders and people of the world, that reconciliation and peace may overcome conflict and oppression: Lord, in your mercy,

For the hungry in body or spirit, that they may be fed: Lord, in your mercy,

For the sick and those in pain, for the lonely and the forgotten, for the dying and all who mourn, [and especially for N.], that they may know the full extent of God's love for them: Lord, in your mercy,

[Here other intercessions may be offered.]

In thanksgiving for the saints and martyrs and for all the faithful departed who join us at your table of grace: Lord, in your mercy,

O God, into your love we commend ourselves and all for whom we pray, through Jesus Christ our Lord.

EASTER VIGIL A

On this holy night of resurrection and joy, let us pray for the church and the world, saying: Lord, in your mercy, hear our prayer.

O God, we give thanks for the goodness of creation, for the victory of resurrection, and for the grace of redemption. We praise you for leading us from darkness into light, and for bringing us through the waters of death into new life in you. Lord, in your mercy,

That the church, celebrating the resurrection with joy, may bring the light of Christ into the world: Lord, in your mercy,

That the newly baptized, buried and raised with Christ, may grow in trust and hope: Lord, in your mercy,

That our community, renewed this night through word and sacrament, may be strengthened in the covenant of our baptism: Lord, in your mercy,

That the people of the world, remembering the source of creation, may care for the waters of the earth and for all living things: Lord, in your mercy,

That the leaders of nations, knowing their power, may bring peace and justice to the world: Lord, in your mercy,

That all who suffer, recalling the mystery of Christ crucified and risen, may be comforted: Lord, in your mercy,

[Here other intercessions may be offered.]

In thanksgiving for the saints and martyrs, for the witnesses of the resurrection, and for all who have passed over from the darkness of death into the glorious light of Christ: Lord, in your mercy,

In joy and faith and hope, we commend ourselves and all for whom we pray to the mercy of God, through Jesus Christ, our risen Lord.

EASTER DAY A
THE RESURRECTION OF OUR LORD A

In the power of the resurrection, let us pray to the Lord, saying: Lord, have mercy.

For the whole bright earth, so lovingly created yet so compassionately redeemed, that it may speak again of the glory and majesty of God, let us pray to the Lord.

For all nations and peoples of the earth, to whom God shows no partiality, that all may be transformed by mercy to live together in hope, let us pray to the Lord.

For the holy church, whose life is hid with Christ in God, that in all its diversity witness may be made to one Lord, one faith, one baptism, let us pray to the Lord.

For all in high places of authority, for whom Christ was put to death and was raised, that they may be led to govern with equity and justice, bringing life to those in the shadow of death, let us pray to the Lord.

For all who have been baptized and given the garments of light, that they, with the whole church, may be witnesses to the gospel in daily life, let us pray to the Lord.

For all captives, prisoners, and those condemned to die, with whom the Holy One shares suffering and abandonment, that they may find strength, freedom, and forgiveness, let us pray to the Lord.

For all who suffer in mind, body, or soul, for whom Christ is risen with healing in his glorious wings, that they may be comforted, let us pray to the Lord.

For all who have died and for all who grieve, that in Christ who triumphs over death they may find light perpetual and blessed assurance, let us pray to the Lord.

For all gathered in this assembly, that we, like Mary and Peter and John, may see the tomb empty, and joyfully believing, walk in newness of life, let us pray to the Lord.

[Here other intercessions may be offered.]

Rejoicing in the risen presence of our Lord, we commend all for whom we pray and ourselves to Christ, to whom we give laud and praise now and forever.

SECOND SUNDAY OF EASTER A

Let us who have been born anew to a living hope through the resurrection pray for the church, the world, and all in need, saying: Lord, hear us in your mercy.

For a new birth of peace on the earth among all human families and nations, that hatred and violence and war may cease, we pray:

For the whole body of Christ and all who bear his holy name, and for bishops, clergy, and all who offer ministries, that we may serve Christ with glad and generous hearts, we pray:

For this nation and all nations of the world, that those who lead may know truth and practice integrity, that all peoples may grow together in concord, we pray:

For all in mental anguish and whose faith is racked by doubt, that they may be led with Thomas the apostle to cry out, "My Lord and my God," we pray:

For those imprisoned unjustly by force, that they may be liberated and not be abandoned to the dominion of death, we pray:

For all gathered here out of love for Christ, that we may know the gospel as an inheritance which is imperishable, undefiled, and unfading, we pray:

For those having died in faith [especially N.] and for all the dying [especially N.], that they may know the love of God who has raised Christ up, having loosed the pangs of death, we pray:

[Here other intercessions may be offered.]

Bind us in love to those for whom we pray this day, and to one another in genuineness of faith, more precious than gold, that Christ may be present in all we do and say. So may your life be praised, today and all days.

THIRD SUNDAY OF EASTER A

Let us who journey on the way with Christ, risen and ever-present in mystery, pray for the world with all our heart and mind, saying: Lord, hear our prayer.

For the church universal and for this community of faith, that we may wholeheartedly devote ourselves to the apostolic teaching, to common life, to the breaking of bread and the life of prayer, let us pray to the Lord.

For all nations and people of this wide earth, that we may be delivered from human devices of oppression, and from false idols and futile ways, let us pray to the Lord.

That all who grieve or who are desperate or haunted by violence may know the hidden strength of Christ present, let us pray to the Lord.

For the homeless, those without bread, those tempted by vengeance and driven to rage, that they may find refuge and strength in the one who walks with them, let us pray to the Lord.

For the children of calamity, and for our own children, that they may come to know and to claim the promises of God to all generations, near and far off, let us pray to the Lord.

[Here other intercessions may be offered.]

Preserve us all, O Lord, and take us home to your heart, so that all our lives may be woven together in prayer and praise, through Jesus Christ our Lord.

FOURTH SUNDAY OF EASTER A

Gathered in the care of the Good Shepherd and guardian of our souls, let us in trust pray for the church and the world, saying: Lord, have mercy.

For all who serve the holy church of God, who serve tables and who preach and pray, who shepherd the lost and care for those in need, let us pray to the Lord.

For all who are persecuted for the gospel, for all who have been martyred for their witness to the truth, for all in lonely places who rejoice in the hope of the resurrection, and for the blessed community of the saints, living and dead, let us pray to the Lord.

For all in the world who care for the sick, the dying, the hungry and the destitute, the mentally ill and the deformed, let us pray to the Lord.

For victims of rage and sudden violence, especially for abused children and spouses, for political prisoners, victims of extortion, of murder, and of natural catastrophe, let us pray to the Lord.

For all here gathered and our specific needs, that we may come to receive abundant life at God's hand, and at the last to rest in Christ's shepherding love, let us pray to the Lord.

[Here other intercessions may be offered.]

O loving God, we commend to your mercy all who have died and pray that we and all your saints may share life in your eternal dominion. Enable us to know that by Christ's wounds we have been healed, and that by the power of his risen and Spirit-giving life we are empowered to serve you all our days. We pray through Jesus Christ, our risen Lord.

FIFTH SUNDAY OF EASTER A

Empowered by the Lord's promise that he will do whatever we ask in his name, let us pray, saying: We ask this in Jesus' name.

For the church of God and for its leaders, that our lives may be for the glory of God alone, let us pray:

For more vigorous efforts to unite all Christian peoples, lest factions and jealousies prevent the spread of the gospel, let us pray:

For all who exercise the ministry of preaching, that their words may be full of the Spirit and of wisdom, let us pray:

For those among us whose hearts are troubled and anxious [especially N.], that they may find support in our care, let us pray:

For this local community, that our belief in God will be deepened by the word and sacrament we share, let us pray:

[Here other intercessions may be offered.]

God of our Lord Jesus Christ, we bring these and all our needs to you, filled with confidence in the power of Jesus' name. Hear us and answer our prayers in your great wisdom and love. We ask this through Christ who is our risen Lord now and forever.

SIXTH SUNDAY OF EASTER A

Let us now demonstrate the hope that fills our hearts by turning to God in prayer, saying: Lord, hear our prayer.

Empower with your Spirit, O Lord, all ministers of the gospel, that they may preach the word boldly and without apology.

Empower with your Spirit, O Lord, all leaders of nations, that they may be unrelenting in their quest for peace.

Empower with your Spirit, O Lord, all the suffering peoples of this world, especially those who suffer for doing right.

Empower with your Spirit, O Lord, those among us who experience desolation, especially those for whom God seems most remote.

Empower with your Spirit, O Lord, all the sick and the dying [especially N.], that they may find life.

Empower with your Spirit, O Lord, the newly baptized, that they may never cease to praise you for the hope that fills their hearts.

[Here other intercessions may be offered.]

Gracious God, it is in the power of your abundant and life-giving Spirit that we call upon you in prayer. Deepen our hope in your presence and your promise; hear us in your tender love, now and forever.

ASCENSION DAY A

In the power of the Risen Lord who intercedes on our behalf, let us pray, saying: Lord, have mercy.

That we might be your faithful witnesses, even to the ends of the earth, we pray:

That Christians everywhere might ask the Spirit of God to rule their lives, we pray:

That repentance and forgiveness of sins might be preached to the nations, we pray:

That those who are paralyzed by fear or doubt might be healed and renewed, we pray:

That all who are destitute and all who are ill [especially N.] might share in God's good life, we pray:

That we might learn to trust in the immeasurable greatness of God's power at work in us who believe, we pray:

[Here other intercessions may be offered.]

God of our Lord Jesus Christ, as we celebrate the ascension of your Son, teach us to trust that he lives to intercede on our behalf, now and forever.

SEVENTH SUNDAY OF EASTER A

Let us once more cast our cares upon the Lord, saying: To God be glory forever and ever.

For the church of God, especially its members who share in Christ's suffering, that the glory of the Lord might be revealed, we pray:

For the world so loved by God, that the power of God's grace working in us might restore the beauty of its created image, we pray:

For those who glorify God in simple, hidden, and faith-filled ways, we pray:

For those labeled wrongdoer and mischief-maker, that they might be loved without judgment and might enjoy God's life, we pray:

For this local community, that the coming of the Spirit might find us steadfast in prayer and strong in love, we pray:

For all in any pain and for all who sorrow [especially N.], that they might be brought beyond their trouble into the Spirit's peace, we pray:

[Here other intercessions may be offered.]

Good and gracious God, you do infinitely more for us than all we can ask or even imagine. Hear these prayers; be our Savior again, now and forever.

PENTECOST SUNDAY A
DAY OF PENTECOST A

In the power of the Spirit who aids us in our weakness and teaches us to pray, let us offer to God our intercessions, thanksgivings, and the deep yearnings of our hearts, saying: Come, Holy Spirit.

For the church, for bishops, for clergy, and for all the people of God, that they may be made whole and free by the Spirit, and bear witness in every aspect of life to the full force of Christ's resurrection, we pray:

For our world in its brokenness, that the peace of the risen Christ heal the wounds of all victims of injustice and exploitation, and transform the hearts of those who lead the nations and who make public policy, that they may truly become makers of peace, we pray:

That liberal and conservative may be drawn together in truth by the Spirit and come to rejoice in their different gifts and points of view, we pray:

For those weighed down by despair, suffering from addiction, or burdened by illness [especially N.], that they may experience the freedom which the Spirit gives to the children of God, we pray:

[Here other intercessions may be offered.]

In thanksgiving for the departed, and for all who witnessed to us of God's love poured into our hearts by the Spirit, and for the grace to be faithful to all they have been for us, we pray:

Gracious God, receive our prayer; hear our hearts' deep yearnings, yet to be formed into words. Give us the courage to yield ourselves, all that we are and have yet to become, to the transforming motion of your Holy Spirit, and carry out in us and through us your work of new creation. This we pray in the name of Jesus Christ, the risen and living one.

TRINITY SUNDAY A

Bound together in Christ in the communion of the Holy Spirit, let us pray with one heart and mind to our God, saying: Holy Trinity, hear us.

That the love which passes ceaselessly between the Father and the Son in the fellowship of the Holy Spirit may renew and deepen the life of each Christian and draw us all gathered here into your unending life, we pray:

For the leaders of the church [especially N.], and for the leaders of nations [especially N.], that they may discern the ways to overcome divisions and mistrust, and may reflect your unity in every aspect of common life, we pray:

That your self-disclosure in Christ and your enduring presence among us as Spirit may help us to understand both you and ourselves, made in your image and likeness, we pray:

For our families, our households, and our communities, that they may be places of communion and mutual support, which build us up and strengthen us in grace and truth, we pray:

Thankful for our world which you made through Christ, and renewed in the power of his resurrection, that we may be wise and careful stewards of creation, we pray:

In the power of the Spirit who joins our prayer to Christ's enduring intercession, we pray for the sick, the suffering, and all who stand in need [especially N.]. For healing for all the world we pray:

[Here other intercessions may be offered.]

Gracious God, whom Jesus called Abba, Father, accept our prayers this day. By the inner workings of your Spirit, deepen our communion with you, the source and goal of our life, and make us more and more signs of your enduring love. This we pray through Christ, who lives and works with you and the Holy Spirit, one God, now and forever.

THE BODY AND BLOOD OF CHRIST A

Gathered together by the God who always nourishes and sustains us, let us intercede for the needs of all the human family, saying: Lord, have mercy.

For the universal church, many members but one body, that God may gather it together from the ends of the earth, safeguard its unity, and perfect it in love, let us pray to the Lord.

For those who control the wealth and resources of nations, that our provident God may give them loving and generous hearts, so that there may be bread for all the children of the earth, let us pray to the Lord.

For victims of famine and those who hunger for spiritual sustenance, that God may satisfy all those in need and inspire us all in the service of justice and evangelism, let us pray to the Lord.

For this assembly gathered at the table of Christ's word and body, that we may abide in Christ and in communion with each other, and, as his body, bear witness to the truth of his gospel, let us pray to the Lord.

[Here other intercessions may be offered.]

For the faithful departed who were strengthened by the eucharist during their earthly pilgrimage [especially N.], and for all the dead who in life hungered for God, that Christ will raise them up to live forever, let us pray to the Lord.

Good and gracious God, whose compassion embraces all generations and whose love provides for all our needs, accept the prayers of your church, and satisfy as your wisdom knows best the hungers of every human heart. Grant this through Christ our Lord.

NINTH SUNDAY IN ORDINARY TIME A
PROPER 4 A
SECOND SUNDAY AFTER PENTECOST A

Made righteous through faith in Christ, asking that we may be faithful to the gift of God's grace, let us now pray to our God in the power of the Spirit, saying: Lord, hear our prayer.

For the church, that in our prayer we may stand ready, as the Lord wills, to carry out and accomplish the very prayer we utter, let us pray to the Lord.

That the urgency of God's word of blessing or curse will shatter our spirit of ~~equivocation and~~ compromise and our easy toleration of expediency and injustice, let us pray to the Lord.

For those who bear the responsibility of government in every nation, that they may build upon the solid rock of truth and justice, and not upon the sands of self-interest and pride, let us pray to the Lord.

That the word of Christ may become the deepest joy of our hearts, and may move us to deeds which reflect Christ's ministry of reconciliation, let us pray to the Lord.

For all in the human community who cry out because of injustice, oppression, illness, or isolation [especially N.], that we may hear in them the cry of Christ himself suffering in his brothers and sisters, let us pray to the Lord.

[Here other intercessions may be offered.]

For the departed [especially N.], that they may continue to support us with their love in the communion of saints, let us pray to the Lord.

Eternal and compassionate God, receive and fulfill all that we ask according to your will. Give us the grace to welcome your word who is Christ, that we may live grounded on the rock of your love and mercy, now and all our days. We ask this through Christ, our Savior and Redeemer.

TENTH SUNDAY IN ORDINARY TIME A
PROPER 5 A
THIRD SUNDAY AFTER PENTECOST A

In Christ, God reveals to us steadfast love and invites us into mercy. With grateful hearts, let us respond in prayer, saying: O gracious God, hear our prayer.

That we and all men and women of faith, and especially the leaders of the church, may know when propriety and order are overruled by the Spirit and may see the outcast and the insignificant as the true bearers of the word: O gracious God,

For the capacity to endure the lashes of God's ruthless love, and for the patience to be conformed to the pattern of Christ's suffering, that we may know and proclaim the power of the resurrection: O gracious God,

For the world's people in their brokenness and suffering, and for those who make peace and do justice, that they may be strong and courageous in the face of discouragement and opposition: O gracious God,

For those who suffer [especially N.], for the sick [especially N.], for the lonely, for the hungry, for victims of political oppression, that mercy and compassion may transform their sorrow into joy: O gracious God,

For the unemployed and for those demeaned or victimized by their work, that they may find new opportunities for joy and satisfaction: O gracious God,

[Here other intercessions may be offered.]

For all who have died, especially those whose witness has strengthened and encouraged us along the way: O gracious God,

God of steadfast love and mercy, hear our prayers, and receive the secret yearnings of our hearts. Grant our petitions in ways that are best for us and for those for whom we pray, and deepen within us an awareness of your mercy and a willingness to follow Christ, in whose name we pray.

ELEVENTH SUNDAY IN ORDINARY TIME A
PROPER 6 A
FOURTH SUNDAY AFTER PENTECOST A

God has called us to be priests for all peoples, offering to God the world's concerns. Let us then pray for the whole people of God in Christ Jesus, and for all people according to their needs, saying: Lord, in your mercy, hear our prayer.

Blessed are you, our sovereign God: for you do not abandon what you have created, but continue to make your grace known among us. We thank you for those you have chosen to speak your reconciling word in this age, and we pray for the grace to receive it. Lord, in your mercy,

Blessed are you, our caring God: for you hear the cries of the poor, you see the tears in the eyes of all who mourn, you feel the pain of those in anguish, and you come to the side of the lonely. Call your church to compassion and service. Lord, in your mercy,

Blessed are you, our God of peace: for you have bid us to make warfare cease and to place our trust in you who bore us up on eagle's wings. Raise up among us peacemakers, and confound those who trust in chariots and horses. Lord, in your mercy,

Blessed are you, our God of justice: for you desire that all be one. Erase the prejudice and class divisions among us, that together we might share in your vision of harmony. Lord, in your mercy,

Blessed are you, our God of strength: for you do not desire harm, but you favor our health. Give to us [and to N.] necessary measures of health, patience, and hope. Lord, in your mercy,

[Here other intercessions may be offered.]

Into your hands, O God, we commend all for whom we pray, trusting in your mercy, through your Son, Jesus Christ.

TWELFTH SUNDAY IN ORDINARY TIME A
PROPER 7 A
FIFTH SUNDAY AFTER PENTECOST A

Our God, the almighty one, counts the hairs of our head. Let us come before God in confidence, praying for all the world, saying: Lord, in your mercy, hear our prayer.

We thank you this day for the value you have placed upon us by giving us Christ our Savior. Empower us to acknowledge this gift in lives of service. Lord, in your mercy,

We thank you, God in Christ Jesus, that you have answered our fears with love. Give to us the faith to go where others dare not to proclaim the vastness of your love. Lord, in your mercy,

We thank you, God in Christ Jesus, that you are concerned with the frailty of our living. You know our addictions, our divorcings, our doubtings, our escapes. Grant us the wholeness we seek. Lord, in your mercy,

We thank you, God in Christ Jesus, that you aid those who work for justice and peace by giving them courage, vision, and strength. Enlist all people in the struggle for human dignity. Lord, in your mercy,

We thank you, O God, that you favor the poor, the meek, the oppressed, the homeless, and the hungry. Make your compassion contagious that the rich might share with the poor, the strong befriend the weak. Lord, in your mercy,

We thank you, O God, that you know the dangers that lurk among us. We pray for those whom you have called to guard and protect your entire creation, those who work the land, who police the streets, who defend the nations. Strengthen them for their difficult tasks. Lord, in your mercy,

We thank you, O God, that you refresh us with times of leisure and recreation. Renew us that we might further appreciate you, each other, and all that you have made. Lord, in your mercy,

[Here other intercessions may be offered.]

We thank you, God in Christ Jesus, that you are always more willing to listen than we are to pray. Hear the petitions of this assembly; hear the prayers spoken in our hearts; for we pray through your Son, Jesus Christ.

THIRTEENTH SUNDAY IN ORDINARY TIME A
PROPER 8 A
SIXTH SUNDAY AFTER PENTECOST A

Through baptism we have been made alive in Christ Jesus. Let us speak the words of this new life by praying for the whole state of Christ's church and the world, saying: Lord, have mercy.

For the church, that we might be faithful, willing to serve, constant in grace, and receptive to newness, let us pray to the Lord.

For this congregation, that we might be eager to welcome, diligent in prayer, and generous in deed, let us pray to the Lord.

For our nation, town, and neighborhood, that we might be advocates of the lowly, defenders of liberties, and models of justice, let us pray to the Lord.

For those who grieve, those in places of care, those in prison, those who are addicted, those who are despondent, [especially N.], let us pray to the Lord.

For those in dangerous occupations, those who care for the sick, those who work the land, those who engage in commerce, and those who teach, let us pray to the Lord.

For all who travel, who seek rest, who visit family and friends, who enjoy the gifts of creation, let us pray to the Lord.

For our families and for all placed under our care, for our enemies and for those with whom we disagree, and for those who are examples of grace in our lives, let us pray to the Lord.

[Here other intercessions may be offered.]

Yours, O God, is the dominion, the power, and the glory, now and forever.

FOURTEENTH SUNDAY IN ORDINARY TIME A
PROPER 9 A
SEVENTH SUNDAY AFTER PENTECOST A

Come to prayer, all who labor and are heavy laden, and God will give us rest. Come to praise, saying: Lord, hear our prayer.

We thank you for the revelation of your gift of abundant life and for the rest coming to those who put their trust in you. For such life and rest,

We thank you for entrusting us with the message of grace, that we might speak a reconciling word to our age. For such mercy,

We thank you for leading us into the ways of peace and for transforming weapons of war into tools of charity. For such peacemaking,

We thank you for the people of faith who surround us and for the family and friends, teachers and clergy who assist our growth in grace. For such companions through life,

We thank you for the gifts of creation and for wholesome times of recreation. For such times of harmony,

We thank you for those who tend the sick, accompany the frustrated, visit the lonely, comfort the dying, confront the addicted, or minister to any in need. For such attention to human anguish,

We thank you for sustaining all who are oppressed, all who suffer for reasons of conscience, all who are passionate for justice. For such signs of the coming kingdom,

[Here other intercessions may be offered.]

Into your hands, O God, we commend all for whom we pray, trusting in your mercy, through your Son, Jesus Christ.

FIFTEENTH SUNDAY IN ORDINARY TIME A
PROPER 10 A
EIGHTH SUNDAY AFTER PENTECOST A

Lest the Word of God return empty to the heavens, let us turn our hearts to the needs of others and plant the seeds of justice, saying: In mercy, hear us.

For the Christian churches throughout the world, that together we may harvest compassion in an abundance of mercy, we pray:

That leaders of government refuse to worship Mars, the god of war, but rather attend to Christ's call of peace, we pray:

For farmers, harvesters, and migrant workers, and for an end of injustice toward those who work the land, we pray:

That people of the earth may honor and respect the natural resources of the planet, and for an end to the consumerism that encourages ravage, we pray:

For the catechumens in our communities, that fertile in faith they may be a soil rich in receptivity, we pray:

For all the sick [especially N.], and for all the oppressed, that the reign of God will hold sway in all human life, we pray:

[Here other intercessions may be offered.]

Blessed and praised are you, O God, for the word of your mouth. In your mercy, listen to all who call to you in faith. Let your word find root in our lives. We pray in the name of your child Jesus, who lives with you in the power of the Spirit, forever.

SIXTEENTH SUNDAY IN ORDINARY TIME A
PROPER 11 A
NINTH SUNDAY AFTER PENTECOST A

As we reach out our thoughts and our energies beyond the walls of this gathering space, hoping that God's reign may be the deepest desire of every human heart, let us pray, saying: In the Spirit we plead, hear us, O God.

O God, may your dominion grasp us and ravish the hearts of all who claim Christ as Lord. In the Spirit we plead:

O God, make your justice grow in our land, that the victims of this age will find shelter in its branches. In the Spirit we plead:

To you, Abba, we raise our eyes in hope. Inspire those whose decisions influence the lives of others, that they may discern wisely and act compassionately. In the Spirit we plead:

O God, imaginative Creator, bless artists, poets, and writers with the creative touch of your word. Make them avenues of your vision. In the Spirit we plead:

O God, we pray for all the oppressed, all the needy, all in terror, all the sick [especially N.]. Give health and peace to all. In the Spirit we plead:

[Here other intercessions may be offered.]

O God, we pray for the dead [especially N.]. On the last day gather us all into your heavenly realm. In the Spirit we plead:

O Master of might and merciful Judge, in our weakness we turn to you for help. Hear us, and come to our rescue. You have promised to hear our prayers if we raise them in the name of Jesus, and so we do. In Jesus' name we pray.

SEVENTEENTH SUNDAY IN ORDINARY TIME A
PROPER 12 A
TENTH SUNDAY AFTER PENTECOST A

With Solomon and the great sages of our lineage, let us now turn our hearts to God and seek true wisdom, saying: O God, hear our prayer.

For the leaders of religious communities and parishes throughout the earth, as they journey towards truth and clarity, we pray for God's wisdom:

For governmental officials, caught in the arms race, locked in an age of deceit and suspicion, we pray for God's wisdom:

For the sick [especially N.], for the dying victims of incurable disease, for those chained by depressions, fear, and addiction, and for those who minister to them, we pray for God's wisdom:

For the youth of our age in their search for the pearl of identity, we ask for God's wisdom:

For all mothers and fathers [especially N.] who awake today without food for their children, we ask for God's wisdom:

For those who seek and never find, for those who travel without purpose, and for those blind to the needs of others, we ask for God's wisdom:

[Here other intercessions may be offered.]

Astonish us once again, O God, and bring forth from the storeroom of your heart the abundance of wisdom. May all who ask for our prayers know your love, and may we give testimony to your grace in our lives of compassion. In the name of Christ we pray.

EIGHTEENTH SUNDAY IN ORDINARY TIME A
PROPER 13 A
ELEVENTH SUNDAY AFTER PENTECOST A

Who can separate us from the love of God? What can separate us from the love of Christ? Let our hearts now respond to such overwhelming love as we pray together in the Spirit, saying: Hear us, O Lord.

That God will renew the merciful covenant made with us in love, we pray:

That the ministers of the gospel may be people of genuine conversion and prophetic voice, we pray:

That the bread of life may be shared one day by all Christians at a common table of praise, we pray:

For the poor of our world, and for governments called to assist them in their need, we pray:

For the sick and the suffering in our world [especially N.], we pray:

For those preparing for baptism, that they may hear the invitation of God to come to the waters of regeneration and there find abundant life, we pray:

For the newly wedded couples in our community, for expectant parents, and for those who nurture children, that all may be fed at the breasts of a loving God and find strength in lives of service, we pray:

[Here other intercessions may be offered.]

Let us be mindful of the dead [especially N.]. That they may come into the fullness of life, united with God in the communion of the faithful, we pray:

O God, your loving care for us calls for our gratitude. Multiply once again your abundant mercy toward us; renew your covenant with us; and let our hearts overflow with godly love for others. We ask this in the name of Jesus, our Rabbi and Lord, now in the Spirit and forever.

NINETEENTH SUNDAY IN ORDINARY TIME A
PROPER 14 A
TWELFTH SUNDAY AFTER PENTECOST A

for those who endure the storms of this life

We are the ark of the church, at times storm-tossed and frightened. Let us cry out in faith for our own needs and the needs of the world, saying: Lord, save us.

For those churches who are resisting oppression and enduring persecution in the name of the gospel, let us cry out to the Lord.

For the leaders of nations, communities, and households who are faced with terrible choices and whose decisions affect the lives of many, let us cry out to the Lord.

For those caught in addictions of mind or body, for those who feel powerless and sink ever deeper into despair, let us cry out to the Lord.

For those who rely on themselves, for those who struggle to trust in God's beckoning word, for those who know fear before the actions of grace, let us cry out to the Lord.

For all of us who gather at this eucharistic table, weak in faith, faltering in our response to God, let us cry out to the Lord.

[Here other intercessions may be offered.]

O true and faithful God, you are the hope of those who cry out to you. Hear our petitions. Where there is no faith, awaken it; where there is little faith, enlarge it, that one day we may all come to acknowledge Jesus as your Son and the savior of the world. We ask this in his name, who is one with you and the Holy Spirit, God, forever and ever.

TWENTIETH SUNDAY IN ORDINARY TIME A
PROPER 15 A
THIRTEENTH SUNDAY AFTER PENTECOST A

The Canaanite woman pressed upon Jesus her needs and was heard. With expectant faith, let us place before God earnest petitions for ourselves and our world, saying: Lord, have pity on us.

For our world, in need of healing, in search of a savior, yet far from Jesus, let us call out to the Lord.

For the churches and their leaders, at times narrowed by institutional concerns and blind to differing manifestations of faith, let us call out to the Lord.

For those who are troubled by demons of mind and body, for those who must watch others suffer, [and especially for N.,] let us call out to the Lord.

For those whose faith is impelling them beyond the limits of society and the constraints of culture, let us call out to the Lord.

For all of us here present, for those whose faith is known to God alone, and for those intentions we hold deep in our hearts, let us call out to the Lord.

[Here other intercessions may be offered.]

Infinite God, we have no claim to your mercy; yet it is your mercy we so desperately need. Turn your ear toward our supplications, and grant us your healing touch. We ask this with faith in the name of Jesus, who is savior of the world and one with you and the Holy Spirit, one God forever and ever.

TWENTY-FIRST SUNDAY IN ORDINARY TIME A
PROPER 16 A
FOURTEENTH SUNDAY AFTER PENTECOST A

Through the power of God, Peter saw Jesus in spirit and truth. For the power of God to be felt in our own times, let us offer intercessions, saying: Lord, hear us.

For all peoples of the earth and powers of the world who have not yet recognized Jesus as the Christ, let us pray to the Lord.

For the unity of the churches, and for their common witness to the possibility of faith, let us pray to the Lord.

For those who struggle to believe in the earthly manifestations of Christ in the church, in the liturgy, and in daily life, let us pray to the Lord.

For those who suffer at the hands of the church, and for those who are oppressed in the name of God, let us pray to the Lord.

For ourselves, our families, and our communities, who are daily faced with questions of faith, let us pray to the Lord.

[Here other intercessions may be offered.]

Living God, you wish to be among us in your Son and in his church. Hear the petitions we place before you. Increase our faith that we may see your works more clearly; purify our actions that we may reveal your love more surely. We ask this in the name of Jesus, your Son, who lives and reigns with you and the Holy Spirit, one God, forever and ever.

TWENTY-SECOND SUNDAY IN ORDINARY TIME A
PROPER 17 A
FIFTEENTH SUNDAY AFTER PENTECOST A

In today's gospel, Jesus invites us to follow him. As he laid down his life in intercession for the world, let us pray on behalf of people everywhere, saying: Lord, strengthen us.

For all people of faith who struggle to believe in the promise of life amid the clamor of death, let us pray to the Lord.

For the churches who must bear witness to the possibility of taking up the cross and following Jesus, let us pray to the Lord.

For those who are losing their souls in the pursuit of worldly gain, let us pray to the Lord.

For those laying down their lives in faithful dedication to God's call, let us pray to the Lord.

For those who are to die this week, and for their safe passage to the life of the world to come, let us pray to the Lord.

For all here present who will one day be judged by God's standards and meet Christ coming in glory, let us pray to the Lord.

[Here other intercessions may be offered.]

Most high God, your ways are not our ways, yet your ways bear life. Hear the petitions of your assembled people. Pour out on your world the faith to hear your call and the courage to answer it. We ask this in the name of Jesus, who is one with you and the Holy Spirit, one God, forever and ever.

TWENTY-THIRD SUNDAY IN ORDINARY TIME A
PROPER 18 A
SIXTEENTH SUNDAY AFTER PENTECOST A

God's word tells us that those who love their neighbors have fulfilled the law. Out of love and compassion for a broken world, let us pray to the Lord, saying: Lord, have mercy.

For nations crippled by international debt, for nations who must beg and scramble for the necessities of life, for nations whose people live in poverty, let us pray to the Lord.

For all Christians who have more than they need, that taking the Lord's word to heart, they may be content with what is necessary and generously share their surplus with the poor, let us pray to the Lord.

Remembering the children of our own country caught in the cycle of poverty, ignorance, disease, and despair, let us pray to the Lord.

For those in our own [city and] neighborhood who are out of work and out of luck, for broken families, for those crippled by debt, for those at their wit's end, let us pray to the Lord.

[Here other intercessions may be offered.]

Lord, you invited the beggars and the crippled, the lame and the blind, to eat and drink at your table and to feast in your kingdom; and lo, here we are. Grant us the grace to extend to others the same generosity you have shown to us; for you are our Lord, our God forever and ever.

TWENTY-FOURTH SUNDAY IN ORDINARY TIME A
PROPER 19 A
SEVENTEENTH SUNDAY AFTER PENTECOST A

Our God is a God of unity, not of division; of love, not of hate; of forgiveness, not of resentment. With open hearts, bearing the pain of the world, let us beseech the God of love, saying: We beseech you, O Lord.

For our brothers and sisters of every race and nation:
for their safety and well-being,
for the relief of their sufferings,
for the assuaging of their hunger and thirst,
and for the overcoming of enmity,
let us pray to the Lord.

For those peoples we have come to view as enemies:
for the peoples of the Soviet Union and China,
[for the peoples of N. and N.,]
for the healing of hatred and the birth of friendship,
let us pray to the Lord.

For the churches of the world, let us pray:
for the healing of divisions,
for growth in understanding,
for devotion to the truth of the gospel,
for our mutual enrichment,
and for complete communion in the Holy Spirit,
let us pray to the Lord.

For our homes and families:
for an end to feuds,
for release from the cycle of violence,
for the healing of painful memories,
for forgiveness and peace between those who injure,
for patience in bearing with one another,
let us pray to the Lord.

[Here other intercessions may be offered.]

Lord God, your Son made himself the least among us, bore our sins upon the cross, and delivered us from death by his own suffering and dying. Forgive us our sins, by which we have added to the world's pain, and make us instruments of peace and reconciliation, through the same Christ our Lord.

TWENTY-FIFTH SUNDAY IN ORDINARY TIME A
PROPER 20 A
EIGHTEENTH SUNDAY AFTER PENTECOST A

God is a God of tenderness and compassion, slow to anger and rich in mercy, generous and forgiving to all who cry for grace. With confidence, let us turn to our God in prayer, saying: Lord, have mercy.

For people throughout the world who are suffering at this very hour from drought and famine, from economic distress and social disruption, from violence and war, let us pray to the Lord.

For the church throughout the world, that we, together with all our brothers and sisters in Christ, may be effective agents of social transformation and reliable messengers of hope, let us pray to the Lord.

For our own country, that its wealth and power might become a force for peace, rather than conflict; a source of hope, rather than discontent; an agent of friendship, rather than enmity, let us pray to the Lord.

For our own community, and especially for those among us who are dispirited and broken-hearted, who find no hope or meaning or purpose in life, let us pray to the Lord.

For ourselves, that we may have the grace to rejoice with those who rejoice, to weep with those who weep, to grieve for others' losses rather than our own, to be quick to forgive and slow to take offense, let us pray to the Lord.

[Here other intercessions may be offered.]

Lord God, in your presence none of us can boast, and all must ask for mercy; yet your Son has embraced us and called us to share in his labors for the salvation of every man, woman, and child. Grant us the grace to see what needs to be done and the wisdom and resources to do it, through the same Christ our Lord.

TWENTY-SIXTH SUNDAY IN ORDINARY TIME A
PROPER 21 A
NINETEENTH SUNDAY AFTER PENTECOST A

God is a father to those who obey God's word and to those who ignore it. With great humility, then, and with great confidence, let us confide to God the hopes and needs, the pains and the labors of the whole world, saying: Lord, hear our prayer.

For all in this world who do not know Christ as the faithful Son who did the will of his Father and revealed to us his Father's kindness, that God's love may be known among them, let us pray to the Lord.

For the churches of the world, that they might prove in their collective witness and action the obedience to God that they profess, let us pray to the Lord.

For all peoples who claim God as their father: for our Jewish and Islamic brothers and sisters, that they may be at peace with us and rejoice with us to do their Father's will, let us pray to the Lord.

For this country, that our unity might be strengthened by genuine commitment to God's will and by faithful obedience to God's word, let us pray to the Lord.

For traitors and prostitutes, for drug-peddlers and con artists, for all who live in the underworld of our nation or outside the pale of respectability, that they might continue to be the special object of God's love, let us pray to the Lord.

For ourselves, that we might be delivered from all illusion of superiority, from all pretense of righteousness, from all arrogance and hardness of heart, and that we might know the meaning of compassion, let us pray to the Lord.

[Here other intercessions may be offered.]

God, you are a God of mercy, a God who does not deal with us according to our sins nor make your love contingent on our good behavior. Be merciful to your people everywhere, and hear our prayers for those who are in need. We ask this through Jesus Christ our Lord.

TWENTY-SEVENTH SUNDAY
IN ORDINARY TIME A
PROPER 22 A
TWENTIETH SUNDAY AFTER PENTECOST A

The Christian church is the vineyard of the Lord, with all its needs and problems: growing the grapes, making the wine, managing the Lord's work. Let us pray to the Lord of the vineyard, saying: Lord, hear our prayer.

That the fruit of our common prayer and ministry be the eucharisitic wine which will soon unite all in Christ the Vine and make us one, let us pray to the Lord of the vineyard:

That our leaders in both church and state may accept their stewardship and accountability to God, and that there may be a rich harvest, let us pray to the Lord of the vineyard.

That the peace of God which is beyond all understanding may lift from our suffering world its burdens of anxiety, war, violence, oppression, poverty, and disease, and that God's fruitfulness will give life to all in need [especially N.], let us pray to the Lord of the vineyard.

That the Lord's vineyard may quickly extend its healthy branches through the world, sheltering the peoples with Christ's gentleness and loving-kindness, let us pray to the Lord of the vineyard.

That Jesus, the stone which the builders rejected, may be recognized as the keystone of church and creation, let us pray to the Lord of the vineyard.

[Here other intercessions may be offered.]

Lord of the harvest, we pray that our global Christian community may fulfill your Son's prayer and that we may soon be one in the name of Christ as he is in you, his Father, in the Holy Spirit, now and forever.

TWENTY-EIGHTH SUNDAY IN ORDINARY TIME A
PROPER 23 A
TWENTY-FIRST SUNDAY AFTER PENTECOST A

We are invited to the wedding banquet which the Father is preparing for the Son's marriage to the church. Let us pray to the host of the eternal feast, that we may be drawn to the banquet, saying: Lord, hear our prayer.

That all in our community may joyously and fully accept God's invitation, and that our heartfelt response be undeterred by distraction and excuses, let us pray to the King of the feast:

That all who hunger and thirst for the bread and wine of life may be drawn to the meal of fellowship in Christ, let us pray to the Lord of heaven:

That all leaders of the church may recognize that God bids the banquet hall be filled with the rich and the poor, the prominent and the unknown, the healthy and the sick, let us pray to the Host of the wedding feast:

That all leaders of the nations may address the global problem of hunger, and that the hungry may be fed, let us pray to the Giver of good food:

That Christians everywhere, abandoning anxiety, may nourish themselves on the marriage celebration with God and on the eternal feast prepared for all peoples, let us pray to the God of lavish and insistent love:

[Here other intercessions may be offered.]

O Lord, supply our needs fully out of your magnificent riches in Christ Jesus. May all one day appear clothed with amazing grace at your Son's wedding banquet, to whom be glory forever and ever.

TWENTY-NINTH SUNDAY IN ORDINARY TIME A
PROPER 24 A
TWENTY-SECOND SUNDAY AFTER PENTECOST A

Pondering the relationship between our duties to God and our duties as citizens, let us pray for ourselves and for the whole world, saying: Lord, have mercy.

That all in our community may know what is God's and what is Caesar's, and may have the courage so to live, let us pray to the one who alone is Lord:

That as the Lord guided Cyrus for the sake of Israel, God will guide our country, its leaders, and its citizens, that justice and peace will be the signs of our trust in God, let us pray to the one who alone is Lord:

That the leaders of the church, in the spirit of Paul, may preach the gospel not merely in words but in the mighty power of the Holy Spirit, let us pray to the one who alone is Lord:

That each of us, following Jesus, may be truthful, courting no one's favor, but living with simplicity and candor, let us pray to the one who alone is Lord:

That through the faith, love, and constancy of Christians God's name may be made known from the rising to the setting of the sun, let us pray to the one who alone is Lord:

That like the apostles all the people in the church may live their faith and labor in love for the poor, the homeless, the imprisoned, the persecuted, and the sick, and that by God's power the suffering of all may be relieved, let us pray to the one who alone is Lord:

[Here other intercessions may be offered.]

O God, ruler of all, grant that our nation and its citizens may respond to your call, and that we may live out all civic virtues in honesty and integrity. We ask this in the name of Jesus, your Son and our Lord.

THIRTIETH SUNDAY IN ORDINARY TIME A
PROPER 25 A
TWENTY-THIRD SUNDAY AFTER PENTECOST A

Pondering the two great commandments of the law, let us pray together, saying: O Lord of love, hear our prayer.

That the church throughout the world may love you with all its heart and soul and mind, and may exemplify your love in all its life, O Lord of love,

That our country, in all its foreign and domestic policies, may care for aliens and immigrants, the indigent and the oppressed, all victims of economic exploitation, and all poorer and smaller nations, O Lord of love,

That the leaders of the churches, with insight and fidelity, may practice love and compassion for all in need, [especially for N.], for all who live in misery, and for all outcasts of society, O Lord of love,

That like the Thessalonians, our community may live in the faith and joy of the Holy Spirit, O Lord of love,

That the wealth of our land may enable us to live in just stewardship of the earth's goods, in care for our natural resources, and in compassion for the needy, O Lord of love,

[Here other intercessions may be offered.]

O God, you care for the widow and the orphan, and you hear the cry of the poor. Listen also to our cry; change our hearts of stone into hearts of flesh with which to love you in truth and for your sake to show compassion on all your creatures. We ask this in the name of Jesus Christ our Lord.

THIRTY-FIRST SUNDAY IN ORDINARY TIME A
PROPER 26 A
TWENTY-FOURTH SUNDAY AFTER PENTECOST A

In confidence that our prayers will be heard and answered, let us address God with boldness and in trust, praying that God's will may be done here and throughout the world, saying: In your mercy, O God, hear our prayer.

We pray for the baptized everywhere and for those preparing for holy baptism, that they may be strong, resolute and faithful as they await the coming of the resurrected Christ. In your mercy, O God,

We pray for the church throughout the world, that it may fulfill its holy task, drawing all people into the family of the redeemed and showing the world the way to peace and justice. In your mercy, O God,

We pray for the leaders of all the nations of the world, that they may renounce war and all which makes for war, giving priority to peace and to that which makes for peace. In your mercy, O God,

We pray for the hungry, the homeless, those who are denied dignity, and those who have no hope, that human compassion will improve their condition and that national compassion will remove the causes of their suffering. In your mercy, O God,

We pray for the sick [especially N.]; for the hospitalized [especially N.]; for those in childbirth [especially N.]; and for all who suffer in mind or body, that they may be granted wholeness and health. In your mercy, O God,

[Here other intercessions may be offered.]

We pray for the dying, that love and loving care may surround them as they prepare for their final journey home. In your mercy, O God,

We place these petitions before you, merciful God, in the name of Jesus Christ, who assures us that if we ask we shall receive, and in response to our baptism, desiring to be used by you as you give answer to our prayers; through Christ our Savior.

THIRTY-SECOND SUNDAY IN ORDINARY TIME A
PROPER 27 A
TWENTY-FIFTH SUNDAY AFTER PENTECOST A

Through baptism, God has made us the people of hope. Our hope is in God and our help comes from God. Since God promises to make all things new, let us offer our cares and concerns to God, saying: O God, who is our hope, hear our prayer.

Gracious Creator, ruler of the universe, we know neither the day nor the hour when the Lord Christ shall return to claim the faithful. Through your saving and sustaining grace, enable us to remain in readiness and to welcome his appearing. O God, who is our hope,

Eternal Creator, author of unity, bind your people together into one holy church. Remove the barriers that separate Christian from Christian, and enable all the baptized to offer common praise to you and common witness to the world. O God, who is our hope,

Merciful Creator, source of all compassion, look with pity upon our world. Help us overcome the ravages of war, disease, hunger, and injustice ; give dignity and well-being to all the human family. Visit us with your love; grant us peace; point us to the way that leads to fulfillment and sufficiency for all. O God, who is our hope,

Almighty Creator, protector of all life, we plead with you to grant healing and wholeness to the sick [especially N.]. Lay upon them your hand of mercy; renew and restore them, giving them cause to proclaim and praise your name. O God, who is our hope,

[Here other intercessions may be offered.]

Divine Creator, perfecter of all life, behold the dying, who no longer await the return of the bridegroom, but rush to meet him through their death. Grant them peace at the last and welcome them into your heavenly dominion. When our last hour shall come, look not on our sins but accept us on the merits of our gracious redeemer, Jesus Christ. O God, who is our hope,

Accept the prayers of your people, O God. Assure us anew that you give heed to our cries and that you respond to our petitions according to your divine will. Through Jesus Christ our Savior we pray.

THIRTY-THIRD SUNDAY IN ORDINARY TIME A
PROPER 28 A
TWENTY-SIXTH SUNDAY AFTER PENTECOST A

The day of the Lord is soon upon us, a day not of wrath but of salvation. As children of the light and of the day, let us await the coming of the Lord in prayer on behalf of the human family around the word, saying: O God, for the sake of Christ, have mercy on us.

Let us pray for those who are not ready for the coming of the Lord, for the unbelieving, the skeptical, the scorners, that they may be brought to faith and rejoice to confess the name of the Lord. O God, for the sake of Christ,

Let us pray for those who use their lips and lives to proclaim the good news of Christ's return, that they may persist in their zeal, empowered and emboldened through the gifts of your Spirit. O God, for the sake of Christ,

Let us pray for those who, with joy and longing, await the return of the Messiah, that they may not grow weary in well-doing, but witness to the immediate and everlasting promise of our holy Redeemer. O God, for the sake of Christ,

Let us pray for those whose lives are marked by hunger and need, grief and loneliness, anger and strife, discord and uncertainty, that each may be assured of the grace and mercy of God. O God, for the sake of Christ,

Let us pray for those who suffer affliction of any kind, that God, their constant companion and champion, may grant them healing and hope and life. O God, for the sake of Christ,

Let us pray for those who are prevented from praying with us, the persecuted and their persecutors, that each may be convinced of the good news of Jesus Christ and respond with faith and commitment. O God, for the sake of Christ,

Let us pray for ourselves, that the Spirit will ready us for the return of our Savior and King, that we may enjoy forever the exhilarating life awaiting the faithful in heaven. O God, for the sake of Christ,

[Here other intercessions may be offered.]

Because you are God, you hear our prayers. Because you are merciful, you promise to answer. We commend to you, merciful God, ourselves and those for whom we pray, through the crucified and risen Lord Jesus Christ.

Let us pray to God, the Father of our Lord Jesus Christ, for the whole church and for all the world, saying: Direct our hearts to keep your law: Lord, have mercy.

Make your church faithful to your word, not seeking to satisfy human expectations but clinging solely to your will and command. Direct our hearts to keep your law:

Make your people listen to the words of the prophets you send, that we may not stray from the paths you have set for us to walk in. Direct our hearts to keep your law:

Make our country a blessing to all the nations of the earth by seeking justice above all things, and lead us in the paths of peace. Direct our hearts to keep your law:

Teach us to pray earnestly night and day that the distressed and afflicted may find comfort. [Especially we pray for N..] May we endure in faith unto the end. Direct our hearts to keep your law:

We beg you by your great might to transform the hunger and hatred and violence which surround us into birthpangs of the new age. Direct our hearts to keep your law:

Make each of us increase and abound more and more in love to one another and to all people and so prepare for the coming of our Lord Jesus Christ. Direct our hearts to keep your law:

When we fail to be your witnesses, recall us to our baptism, cover us with the robe of Christ's righteousness, and increase our faith in Christ our Redeemer, that with renewed resolution we may set out again to walk in your ways. Direct our hearts to keep your law:

[Here other intercessions may be offered.]

Holy and righteous God, we offer you our thanks and praise on behalf of all your people, and we join with all creation in looking with joyful hope to the coming of our Lord Jesus Christ, who shall rule the world with justice and mercy, through whom we offer our prayers and intercessions to you in the unity of the Holy Spirit, now and forever.

LAST SUNDAY, CHRIST THE KING A
PROPER 29 A
CHRIST THE KING A

Through baptism we have been raised with Christ, ordained to a royal priesthood, and made citizens in a holy nation. As faithful priests serving the King of kings, let us intercede for all the world, saying: In the name of Jesus our King, hear our prayer.

Almighty God, sovereign majesty, as your humble priests we pray for all your children who do not confess you as Lord. Enable us to live the good news convincingly, that all may inherit life eternal in the kingdom of heaven. In the name of Jesus our King,

Almighty God, ruler of all nations, cause the leaders of nations to recognize your sovereignty and to accept your gracious rule. Make them proponents of peace and lovers of justice. Crown each ruler with compassion, that all peoples may live in peace. In the name of Jesus our King,

Almighty God, merciful monarch, look with pity on all who suffer: those with incurable disease, those unjustly imprisoned, those denied dignity, the hungry, those without shelter, those who live without hope. Direct us toward them, that their royalty may be reclaimed and their lives celebrate your grace. In the name of Jesus our King,

Almighty God, Lord of the church, we pray for your holy catholic church on earth. Gather all who bear the name of Christ into one vigorous, fruitful community of faith, that the world may see one King of glory and one kingdom of grace. In the name of Jesus our King,

Almighty God, benevolent judge, we pray for all your people gathered here to seek your grace. By your mercy, prepare us for the day of judgment, that we may accept it as a rich and royal gift for the eternal pleasure of the faithful. In the name of Jesus our King,

68 *Last Sunday in Ordinary Time, Christ the King A*
    Proper 29 A
    Christ the King, Last Sunday after Pentecost A

[Here other intercessions may be offered.]

Grant these petitions, O God, according to your perfect will, that your holy name be praised and proclaimed until that day when all the faithful shall gather before your throne in heaven, through the merits of Christ the King.

SUNDAYS, MAJOR HOLY DAYS, AND SOLEMNITIES,

CYCLE B

FIRST SUNDAY OF ADVENT B

At the beginning of this Advent season, let us offer our prayers to God, saying: Lord, have mercy.

That our gracious Savior may rouse us from sleep and make us attentive to the nearness of his presence, let us pray to the Lord.

That we may discover God's word in every sound of this world, God's touch in every human embrace, and God's love in every gesture of self-sacrifice among us, let us pray to the Lord.

That divine energy and holy grace may bring our hearts to vigilance and make us see with uncovered eyes the Christ who suffers in his people's agonies, let us pray to the Lord.

That we may come to recognize in our holy assembly gathered for prayer that Jesus the Christ is with us here to make our songs of praise and pleading his own, let us pray to the Lord.

That God's coming into the days and years of our human history may be always new, always brimming with light to drive all darkness away, let us pray to the Lord.

[Here other intercessions may be offered.]

Make ready our hearts for your coming, O Lord, and receive our prayers in the name of the one who comes, our gracious Savior, Jesus, the Christ.

SECOND SUNDAY OF ADVENT B

*In joy at the nearness of the Christ, let us offer our prayers to God,
saying: Lord, hear our prayer.*

May the power of God's holy presence clear a path through the
rubble of broken lives and hearts to make our world and all of
us a new creation. For this let us pray to the Lord.

May our gracious God be always for us a shepherd to console
and comfort us, to nourish all our deep hungers, and to make
us live in peace forever. For this let us pray to the Lord.

May we come to find in the desert of our lives the gift of
forgiveness and the waters of a new Jordan that bring cleansing
refreshment. For this let us pray to the Lord.

May the God of John the Baptist and our God continue to raise
up holy prophets in our midst who will tell the good news of
saving rescue for all people. For this let us pray to the Lord.

May the God who is our comfort hear the cries of all in need
[especially N.]. For this let us pray to the Lord.

[Here other intercessions may be offered.]

May the God who is our future in the gift of Jesus Christ hold
us always in the embrace of faithful love and bring us to new
heavens and a new earth. For this let us pray to the Lord.

*Recall us to our baptism, O Lord, and hear our cries for ourselves and
for the whole world, for we pray in the name of the one who came,
Jesus Christ our Lord.*

THIRD SUNDAY OF ADVENT B

Pleading for God's gift of a renewing Spirit, let us offer our prayers to God, saying: Lord, hear our prayer.

That our lives may be songs of praise and thanksgiving rising from joyful hearts and proclaiming in every word we speak and gesture we make that God fills us with holy presence, let us pray to the Lord.

That all those in our world held in captivity or any form of slavery may find liberation from the chains that bind them and new freedom for their hearts, let us pray to the Lord.

That we may accept with courage God's anointing of our lives to share in the divine mission of rescue for the world, bringing justice and joy to all peoples, let us pray to the Lord.

That we may reverently offer in service to the world the ministry of light which we hold in fragile human hands, this sharing in the saving work of Christ the Light, let us pray to the Lord.

That the mercy of God which lasts from age to age may wash over us and bless us and stir up in us the bold courage to be its faithful prophets in our world, let us pray to the Lord.

[Here other intercessions may be offered.]

Send the Spirit of Jesus upon us, O God, that we may be your songs of peace and joy in this world. We pray in the name of the one who is our peace and joy, Christ our Lord.

Rejoicing with Mary that the word comes among us, let us offer to God our prayers, saying: Lord, hear our prayer.

May we find in Mary, the servant of the Lord, the model of our heart's willing surrender to God's call. For this let us pray to the Lord.

May we discover in true spiritual virginity the richness of what God alone can do to make Christ come alive in Mary, in us, and in all the world. For this let us pray to the Lord.

May the God of mystery who dwells in unapproachable light draw us more and more deeply into the path of divine wisdom beyond all human expectation. For this let us pray to the Lord.

May our assembly of disciples be a womb and a place for the shaping of Christ by God's power, so that we may give birth to Christ from the womb of our community for the world. For this let us pray to the Lord.

May our deepest hearts find strength in the gift of blessed hope that what God has begun to do in our world and in all our persons by Christ's saving work will be brought to its fullness by our Savior. For this let us pray to the Lord.

May we remember before God all who are in any need and who cry for the presence of God [especially N.]. For this let us pray to the Lord.

[Here other intercessions may be offered.]

Call us to yourself, O God, as you called Mary, that we may be formed into a dwelling of holiness, giving life to all the peoples of the world through Mary's son, Jesus Christ our Lord.

CHRISTMAS MASS AT MIDNIGHT B
CHRISTMAS DAY I B
THE NATIVITY OF OUR LORD 1 B

Brothers and sisters, on this most holy night of our Lord's birth, that we may find peace, joy, and contentment in this holy season, let us pray for ourselves and all those in need of our prayers, saying: Lord, hear our prayer.

For the church of Christ, that it may faithfully proclaim the good news of salvation and may care for the needs of God's people in all corners of the world, we pray to you, O Lord.

For peace in our troubled world, that the darkness of war and injustice may be replaced by the light of peace and love, we pray to you, O Lord.

For all those in need of our prayers: the homeless; the unemployed; the hungry; those who are hospitalized [especially N.]; those who are imprisoned in body or soul; and all those for whom this season is one not of joy but of trial and sadness, we pray to you, O Lord.

For the sick [especially N.], that their illnesses may be turned into health and their sorrow into rejoicing, we pray to you, O Lord.

For those who labor this night on behalf of others: doctors and nurses, police officers and firefighters, gas station attendants, bus and taxi drivers, and all those whose work prevents them from sharing this evening with those they love, we pray to you, O Lord.

[Here other intercessions may be offered.]

In thanksgiving we remember the lives of those who have gone before us in the faith [especially your servant N.]. That we, like them, may remain faithful to the end and live forever in the light of your eternal glory, we pray to you, O Lord.

Mighty God, mercifully hear the prayers of the people you have chosen as your own. Give us zeal in our ministries and joy in our work, through Jesus Christ our Lord.

CHRISTMAS MASS DURING THE DAY B
CHRISTMAS DAY III B
THE NATIVITY OF OUR LORD 2 B

Our Lord Jesus Christ, word become flesh, commanded us to pray for one another. Let us therefore pray for God's people everywhere, according to their own specific needs, saying: Lord, in your mercy, hear our prayer.

Eternal God, bless your holy church, that it may boldly proclaim the good tidings of salvation to all the ends of the earth. Lord, in your mercy,

Bless your servants in this congregation, that nourished by your word and holy sacraments we may minister in faithfulness to you and in love to one another. Lord, in your mercy,

Guide the leaders of the world, that they may put aside their own ambitions and strive for peace and justice among the nations. Lord, in your mercy,

Be with those who travel during this holiday season, that their reunions and celebrations may be occasions for joy and that they return safely to their homes and loved ones. Lord, in your mercy,

Gracious God, grant health and wholeness to the sick [especially N.], and give patience and understanding to those who minister to them. Lord, in your mercy,

As you comforted your people by sending your most precious Son, the word of life, comfort those whose lives have been shattered by the loss of a loved one, that their sorrow may be turned to joy. Lord, in your mercy,

[Here other intercessions may be offered.]

In thanksgiving we remember before you, O Lord, those saints who bore witness to the light [especially N.]. Grant that we may persevere in the faith to which we have been called and at the end behold your glory. Lord, in your mercy,

All these things we ask in the name of him who came as the light in the darkness of our world, Jesus Christ our Lord.

HOLY FAMILY B
FIRST SUNDAY AFTER CHRISTMAS B

Brothers and sisters in the faith, God has called us into the family of the church. In the Spirit of Christ, we call out "Abba, Father," asking our creator to hear the prayers we offer, saying: Lord, in your mercy, hear our prayer.

Let us pray for the human family:

Eternal Father, you entrusted to Mary and Joseph the life of your child, Jesus. Strengthen all parents and children in the bonds of love, peace, and faith. Lord, in your mercy,

Let us pray for the household of the church:

Creator of life, make your church a fruitful vine to all who are reborn in the living waters of baptism. May we find ourselves continually nourished and refreshed at the table of Christ's body and blood. Lord, in your mercy,

Let us pray for those who suffer:

Consoler of the afflicted, sustain the homeless and the abandoned. Protect the widow, the widower, the orphan. Comfort those who mourn the dead. [Hear our prayer for N..] Lord, in your mercy,

Let us pray for the families of this community:

God of love, like a mother you nourish us with your grace. Quicken in us the seed of Christ's word, that we might reveal his life to the whole human family. Lord, in your mercy,

[Here other intercessions may be offered.]

Gracious God, may your favor and blessing rest upon the family which you have gathered in the name of your child Jesus. Accept the prayers we offer in his name. So may your love embrace us, now and forever.

SECOND SUNDAY AFTER CHRISTMAS B

The word of God lives among and within us to strengthen and inspire. With confidence let us pray to our God, the Father, with words of hope and faith.

Let us pray for the church of Jesus Christ:

God of light, empower your ministers and people to proclaim your gospel fearlessly wherever darkness obscures human dignity. Lord, in your mercy,

Let us pray for the nations of the world:

God of peace, in your word we recognize the abundance of your enduring love. Grant to this world, marked by division and strife, a thirst for justice perfected in selfless love. Lord, in your mercy,

Let us pray for the hungry and the abandoned:

God of life, strengthen us to serve with joy those who experience the darkness of suffering. [We pray especially for N..] Lord, in your mercy,

Let us pray for all educators:

God of wisdom, in your word we hear the proclamation of your truth. Enlighten all who teach with your Spirit of knowledge and understanding. Lord, in your mercy,

Let us pray for this community of faith:

God of grace, give us hearts filled with love, voices to speak your praise, and lives conformed to the image of your Son. Lord, in your mercy,

Let us pray for the sick and the dying:

God of glory, in your word we receive the promise of life beyond weakness and sorrow. Heal those who call upon you in faith, and reveal your light to those in the shadow of death. [We pray especially for N..] Lord, in your mercy,

[Here other intercessions may be offered.]

Creator of all, you have not abandoned your creation, but have made your dwelling with us in Christ. Hear your faithful people, and grant us the blessings of your mercy, for we make this prayer in the name of Jesus who is Lord forever and ever.

THE EPIPHANY OF OUR LORD B

God has called us out of darkness into the glorious light of the Son. Let us therefore pray for those who do not yet know the light and for all those in need of our prayers, saying: Lord, hear our prayer.

For the church and its ministry to the world, for all bishops and clergy, for missionaries, and for all those who bring the gospel of Jesus Christ to the nations, let us pray to the Lord.

For the nations of the world and their leaders, for all those in authority [especially N.], and for an end to war and oppression, let us pray to the Lord.

For those who have not heard the good news of salvation, for those who have heard but have not believed, and for those who have forsaken their faith, let us pray to the Lord.

For the lonely and destitute, for the victims of injustice and discrimination, for the unloved and the forgotten, let us pray to the Lord.

For the sick in body, mind, and spirit, for the hungry and the homeless, for the dying and the bereaved, and for all those in need of our prayers [especially N.], let us pray to the Lord.

[Here other intercessions may be offered.]

For the saints who have gone before us in the faith and are now at rest [especially N.], and for all the saints on earth who surround us in a great fellowship of love, let us pray to the Lord.

Loving God, hear the prayers of your faithful people, and guide our thoughts and actions, so that your will may be done and your name glorified, through Jesus Christ our Lord.

THE BAPTISM OF OUR LORD B
FIRST SUNDAY AFTER EPIPHANY B

In the waters of baptism, we were called to be God's children and to minister to one another. Let us therefore pray for ourselves, for one another, and for all those in need of our prayers, saying: Lord, in your mercy, hear our prayer.

Let us pray for the church, that it may stand fast in the one faith to which it has been called. [*Silence.*] Lord, in your mercy,

Let us pray for the world, that our conflicts may cease and that peace may reign in this new year. [*Silence.*] Lord, in your mercy,

Let us pray for all Christians who have been baptized into the one family of faith, that our lives reflect the forgiveness and love which was first shown us. [*Silence.*] Lord, in your mercy,

Let us pray for all who are blind to the injustices of our world, that their eyes may be opened and that they may work for an end to oppression and injustice. [*Silence.*] Lord, in your mercy,

Let us pray for the sick [especially N.], that their sickness may be turned to health and that they may once again join us in our work and worship. [*Silence.*] Lord, in your mercy,

[Here other intercessions may be offered.]

Let us pray for the faithful who have gone before us, that we may follow the example of their lives and be reunited with them in the joy of everlasting life. [*Silence.*] Lord, in your mercy,

Omniscient God, you know our thoughts and needs better than we ourselves. Accept the prayers which we now offer, and strengthen us to do your will, through Jesus Christ our Lord.

SECOND SUNDAY IN ORDINARY TIME B
SECOND SUNDAY AFTER EPIPHANY B

Called together as a family of faith from every time and place, we are bidden by God to pray. That we might share our mutual concerns and offer the secrets of our hearts, let us pray, saying: Lord, in your mercy, hear our prayer.

Let us pray for the world; for the leaders of nations, that wisdom and integrity might prevail; for regions torn by conflict, that peace and harmony might be restored: Lord, in your mercy,

Let us pray for the church; for the unity of the body of Christ, that needless division might cease; for N. our bishop, for N. our clergy, and for all who nurture our life together, that the body may be strengthened and our common life enriched: Lord, in your mercy,

Let us pray for this parish; for our presence in this community, that persons may find here the means to a deeper relationship with God; and for our ministry of reconciliation, that all may find here the forgiveness of God and the acceptance of each other: Lord, in your mercy,

Let us pray for those in need; for the hungry and homeless, that food and shelter might be theirs; for the oppressed and downtrodden, that freedom and dignity might be theirs; for the sick and the infirm [and especially for N.], that health and wholeness might be theirs: Lord, in your mercy,

[Here other intercessions may be offered.]

By your power, dear God, you raised Christ Jesus and in him we too will be raised. Receive our prayers and those of all your saints, that trusting in you all the days of our lives, we may know the fullness of your love and the power of the resurrection; through Jesus Christ our Lord

THIRD SUNDAY IN ORDINARY TIME B
THIRD SUNDAY AFTER EPIPHANY B

As God is moved by the sincerity of our repentance, so too God is pleased by the faithfulness of our prayers. Let us offer our prayers to God, saying: In your mercy, hear us, Lord.

You have called us, O God, to follow you. Give us the grace to listen to your call, to lay aside the things of this world, and to follow you. In your mercy,

You have sent us, O God, into the world to tell the story of your love and faithfulness. Give us a holy zeal for the proclamation of the gospel in this place and in all the world. In your mercy,

You have called, O God, persons of varieties of gifts to serve your church. Bless, we pray, the ministries of musicians and artists, scholars and writers, pastors and teachers, that their work enrich our common life and offer us a glimpse of the life to come. In your mercy,

You gave life, O God, for us and for all people. We remember before you those who are sick [especially N.], those who mourn [especially N.], and those who rejoice [especially N.]. As you have reached out to us in love, so inspire us to be present to those we have named before you. In your mercy,

[Here other intercessions may be offered.]

As we are faithful in prayer, O God, so make us faithful in following you, that loving and serving you all the days of our lives, we may know the joy of the resurrection and may look with longing for your coming in power; through Jesus Christ our Lord.

FOURTH SUNDAY IN ORDINARY TIME B
FOURTH SUNDAY AFTER EPIPHANY B

As the people gathered in Capernaum to hear Jesus' words, so too have we come together to hear God's word. Let us boldly offer our prayers to God, saying: Lord, have mercy.

For the world in which we live and to which we are called, let us pray to the Lord:

For the nations of the world, and for world peace, let us pray to the Lord:

For the church of Christ, zealous in mission, compassionate in service, let us pray to the Lord:

For this congregation and for our hearing the word, let us pray to the Lord:

For all who labor in the world and in the church, let us pray to the Lord:

For those who are sick, [for N.,] and for those who care for them, let us pray to the Lord:

For the homeless and for the refugees, let us pray to the Lord:

For those with whom we rejoice, [for N.,] and for those whose joy is known only in the secrets of their hearts, let us pray to the Lord:

[Here other intercessions may be offered.]

O God, we commend to your care all for whom we pray, in the confidence that your love for them is greater than anything we can know or imagine. Hear us, through Christ our Lord.

FIFTH SUNDAY IN ORDINARY TIME B
FIFTH SUNDAY AFTER EPIPHANY B

Jesus went through Galilee preaching and healing and showing compassion to those in need. As God comes no less today to those for whom we pray, let us offer our prayers to God, saying: Lord, in your mercy, hear our prayer.

Creator of all, look with favor upon the peoples of the world. In your mercy, give to all people the necessities of a dignified life. Lord, in your mercy,

Ruler of creation, instill wisdom and understanding among the leaders of nations. Guide them into ways of justice and peace. Lord, in your mercy,

Lord of the church, gather us all into one holy communion. Give us the courage to look to you alone as the source of our unity. Lord, in your mercy,

Great Physician, bring healing to all who suffer in body, mind, or spirit. We pray for those we know and love, [especially for N.] and for those known only to you. Inspire us to care for your gifts of healthy bodies and minds. Lord, in your mercy,

Spirit of the living Christ, fill us with expectation and eager longing for the coming of that day when no one will suffer, but when all will be gathered together in heavenly joy and eternal prosperity. Lord, in your mercy,

[Here other intercessions may be offered.]

All this we ask, O God, in the name of Christ, who died and rose for us, and whose coming in glory we await. Accept our prayers and praises, through Christ our Lord.

SIXTH SUNDAY IN ORDINARY TIME B
SIXTH SUNDAY AFTER EPIPHANY, B
PROPER 1 B

Having heard the cleansing, restoring word of God, let us offer our prayers for the world, the church, and ourselves, saying: We pray to you, Lord Christ.

O Jesus Christ, who looked with pity on the leprous man and reached out and touched him and made him whole, bring your great healing to the great hurt of our world:

for your peace where there is war, or the threat of war, or the steady preparation for it,

for relief for victims of political folly and of natural disaster,

for comfort for all who cry for help, quite sure that no help is at hand,

and for all those who stand ready to be part of your answer to these petitions:

We pray to you

for all those who have been isolated by illness, or old age, or by an uncaring society,

for those who are shunned and pushed to the edge of the community,

and for those who are institutionalized, that you grant them your nearness:

We pray also

for all who see the abandoned and for all who remember the forgotten,

for strength and perseverance for those who serve,

for all in any need [especially N.],

and for wisdom for us all to create a society more heedful of all its members:

We pray to you for all Christian people,
    for deliverance from the willfulness that sets the terms of
our own healing and stumbles at the simplicity of faith,
    and for courage and steadfastness in the demands that the
world places on faith and obedience:

[*Here other intercessions may be offered.*]

Let us remember those who have died.

*Dear God, we ask, scarcely knowing what and how to ask. You know
the needs we know and the deeper needs we hardly guess. Grant us
what is required for the life to which you call us, not because we ask
wisely or well, but because of the boundless compassion you have made
known to us in Jesus Christ our Lord.*

SEVENTH SUNDAY IN ORDINARY TIME B
SEVENTH SUNDAY AFTER EPIPHANY B
PROPER 2 B

*We have heard God's voice saying through the ancient prophet, "I am
doing a new thing." As we celebrate the new thing done in Jesus
Christ, let us pray for a new thing to be done, saying: We pray to you,
O Lord.*

O God, we pray for our world,
    so resourceful in solving small matters,
    so helpless against self-destruction,
    so set in weary habits of folly.
Bring to the world you love a fresh touch of your life-giving
Spirit. For a way in the wilderness and rivers in the desert,

We pray for those whose skill and training is at work for the
human good:
    for healers of the soul, who say "Your sins are forgiven,"

for healers of the body, who say "Rise and walk,"
for those who relieve the pain of unjust social orders,
for those who struggle against ancient ills of mind, body
or society. For a way in the wilderness and rivers in the desert

We pray for the church, the people you have formed and called
to be a voice of your everlasting praise.
You have promised that you will not remember our sins
grant that we may not remember them against ourselves.
You have established the church in Christ; grant that we
remember in whom we are established.
You have given the guarantee of your Spirit; grant that we
do not quench the Spirit. For a way in the wilderness and
rivers in the desert,

We pray for ourselves,
that your own ever-fresh life may quicken and heal our
inner weariness,
and that we find our truest life by finding yours. For a way
in the wilderness and rivers in the desert,

[Here other intercessions may be offered.]

Let us remember before God those who have died.

*Everlasting God, you have given Jesus Christ as your "Yes" to us
Grant that in the "no" that we hear around us and within, we may
hold in life and death to that faithful yes, Jesus Christ, through whom
we utter our Amen to your glory.*

EIGHTH SUNDAY IN ORDINARY TIME B
EIGHTH SUNDAY AFTER EPIPHANY B
PROPER 3 B

*As a people bound to God in covenant, chastened and set free, let us
pray for the needs of the world and the church, saying: Hear our
prayer, O Lord.*

O God, our human agreements are flawed;

    they set group against group, they oppress some and favor others, they do not last.

    You have called us into your covenant, saying, "You will be my people."

    You have betrothed us to yourself in righteousness, justice, love, mercy, and faithfulness.

    That your Spirit may bring all people ever more fully into that enduring covenant of freedom and peace,

Establish peace, and strengthen those who work for it.

    Bring justice and liberty, and give courage to those who decry injustice and oppression.

    Grant wisdom to those who make the decisions on which the common well-being depends [especially N.].

    That your Spirit may help us to shape a more just and equitable society,

Grant that the church may live out your covenant, not as a legal obligation, but as a gracious gift of the Spirit;

    grant the church wisdom to recognize the new life that is of the Spirit and not to seek to confine it in old forms;

    grant it discernment to know the passing attractions that are not of the Spirit, and to dismiss them.

    That your Spirit may give joy to all Christians as they do their appointed tasks,

Let us pray for those who are sick or suffering, those who are troubled, and those in need. [Especially we pray for N.] That all may find their needs met in Christ,

[Here other intercessions may be offered.]

Let us remember those who have died [especially N.].

Lord Jesus, your coming in Galilee was as a continual marriage banquet. Preserve us from our carelessness and the boredom that shields us from the terror and despair that lurk within. Grant us a vision of the glory at the heart of things that was revealed in your life, your cross, your resurrection, and your living with the Father and the Holy Spirit, one God, now and ever.

LAST SUNDAY AFTER EPIPHANY B
TRANSFIGURATION OF OUR LORD B

The word of God calls us to see that all the places and occasions of the world, even places of sorrow and death, are transfigured by the presence of the glory of God in Christ Jesus. Let us now call to mind all who are in any need and commend them to God's transforming care, saying: O merciful God, hear our prayer.

For those who are alone, for widows and widowers and orphans, and for the divorced, O merciful God,

For the imprisoned, for those whose only home is the streets, and for those caught by addiction, O merciful God,

For the hungry, for those who cannot feed their children, and for the unemployed, O merciful God,

For refugees, for the victims of warfare, and for those held in poverty by racial discrimination, O merciful God,

For the people of our nation, our city, and our community, O merciful God,

For artists and writers, and for all who think on the edge of society, O merciful God,

For preachers and teachers of the light-bearing word of Christ, O merciful God,

For the church and its leaders, formed by the life-giving word of Christ, O merciful God,

For this assembly, feeding on the word of Christ, O merciful God,

[Here other intercessions may be offered.]

With Moses and Elijah and all the people of God, with the church throughout the ages bearing witness to the great light of God shining in dark places, we commend to you all for whom we pray, O merciful God, through Jesus Christ our Lord.

ASH WEDNESDAY B

The prophet urges the people of faith to return with weeping, fasting and chastened heart, for God is gracious and merciful. At the opening of this lenten season let us intercede for a sinful world, a sinful church, and for ourselves, saying: Lord, in your mercy, hear our prayer.

O righteous God, we sin against you, against one another, and against ourselves. Yet over against our sins you have set the eternal Christ in whom you have entered the human lot, reconciling the world to yourself.
> We confess our sin with sorrow, but not despair.
> We claim your abounding grace. Lord, in your mercy,

Our world takes its own way, heedless of your will.
> We exploit and diminish others,
> we threaten your good creation. Grant that in the accelerating crises of our time, your prophetic word may be heard, calling for a turning-about, and that there may be a new beginning of doing justly, loving peace, honoring truth, and walking humbly with you. Lord, in your mercy,

We pray for all victims of our rapacious social order:
> for those scarred by new and old wars,
> for refugees, and those hungry and in despair,
> for those harmed by lies and blighted by false values;
> for the poor and the homeless, and for all those who have no access to the world's abundant resources. We confess our part in destructive patterns of thought and action. Awaken us to bring about change for the well-being of those we know and those many more we do not know, but are bound to by bonds of your making. Lord, in your mercy,

Your church is a people of divided mind,
> naming the name of Christ, but failing that name. Grant that this season of Lent may be for us a summons to repent and return, for now is the acceptable time, and now is the day of salvation. Lord, in your mercy,

[Here other intercessions may be offered.]

We remember those who have died, but who are yet one with us in your everlasting love [especially N.].

O God, it is our burden and our glory to know our sin and to rue it. But you are greater than our hearts and know all things. Your prevailing love for us, while we were yet sinners, has been declared in Jesus. When the terms of life seem too much to be borne, hold not our sins up against us, but hold us up against our sins. We pray through Christ our Lord.

FIRST SUNDAY IN LENT B

We are baptized to lift up, day by day, all the needy world to God. Let us pray for all who are in need, saying: Have mercy, O Lord.

For the church, that all who have found God's promise in the waters of baptism may enter gladly into the testing time of Lent, we pray:

For the church, that the catechumens, called to be ready for Easter baptism, may walk with us these forty days and know both Satan's testing and God's reign, we pray:

For our world, that all living creatures may find goodness on the earth, our home, where life and death may both be God's blessing, we pray:

For deliverance, that in the wastelands made by our greed and indifference we may fast from evil and grow hungry for justice, we pray:

For ourselves in this assembly, that we may strain forward toward Easter, caring for our sick and needy, remembering our dead, believing in our every deed the good news, we pray:

For all those who have claim to our intercession, we pray:

[Here other intercessions may be offered.]

God of wild beasts and of angels, of waters and wilderness, remember us; remember all whom we remember; remember the covenant you made with every living creature, for that is our bond with you now and forever.

SECOND SUNDAY IN LENT B

Jesus Christ intercedes for us at all times. Together let us remember and pray to God through Christ, saying: Have mercy, O Lord.

For the church, that the fasting of these forty days may clear away much that is needless and so open our eyes to the bright glory of the cross, we pray:

For the church, that those baptized at Easter will learn from us to read and ponder and cherish the scriptures, we pray:

For the children of Abraham, Isaac, and Jacob, that the Jewish people may find blessing and a zeal for justice in their covenant with God, we pray:

For all who suffer want, that God in mercy may turn our hearts toward one another and bring us to end our faithless reliance on weapons, war, and the threat of war, we pray:

For prisoners, that all who are bound in body may find such a strength of spirit to lift up all of us, we pray:

For ourselves, that this church may walk both as burdened and as free as Jesus, we pray:

[Here other intercessions may be offered.]

For all who have died, that they be at peace, we pray:

God, whose ways are beyond our knowing or approving, place the world's troubles ever in our plain sight, and be yourself in our seeing and in our praying. We ask this always through Christ our Lord.

THIRD SUNDAY IN LENT B

Gathering all that commands our prayers, let us intercede with our gracious God, saying: Have mercy, O Lord.

For the church, that God's commandments may be ever close to us, wonderful to ponder and life-giving to keep, we pray:

For the church, that those who will be baptized at Easter may be drawn to the folly and weakness of God in Christ crucified, we pray:

For our divided and restless world, that those who hold power over others may be troubled and transformed by the demands of justice, we pray:

For children, that infants and young people of every nation may have food and learning, and that they may love their world, we pray:

For this gathered community, that the solemn brightness of Lent may open our eyes to these times, their folly and their worth, we pray:

[Here other intercessions may be offered.]

For the dead, especially those who held to and handed on God's commandment until our day, that they may be at peace, we pray:

Jealous and merciful God, remember us and all those whom we hold in our hearts. In these forty days teach us to do the work of our baptism and so daily to raise to you the needs of the world. Grant this through Christ our Lord.

FOURTH SUNDAY IN LENT B

Embraced by God's word, let us intercede for all those in need, saying:
Have mercy, O Lord.

For the church, that our lenten hunger may be for justice, and our thirst for deeds of justice, we pray:

For the church, that all those to be baptized at Easter may see through the dazzling attractions of sin and rejoice only in God's marvelous gift, we pray:

For the community of nations, that the worth of every life may compel us on the way to solidarity and peace, we pray:

For exiles and refugees, that all who are homeless because of war or hunger, because of the greed or hatred of others, because of disabilities, may find places of rest and kindness, we pray:

For those who struggle with addictions, that they may find strength and love for the simple gifts of God, we pray:

For this assembly, God's handiwork, that our steps be directed in ways of peace that lead us to the side of those the world despises, and that we name these rejected ones our brothers and sisters, we pray:

[Here other intercessions may be offered.]

God, full of goodness and open to weakness, remember all whom we remember, and remind us of all whom we would forget. We ask this through Christ our Lord.

FIFTH SUNDAY IN LENT B

The hour has come; now is the time to glorify God's name. Let us intercede for the church and for all God's creation, turning to God and saying: Lord, your kingdom come.

You are our God:
may those who are poor and those who are rich, those near and those far, welcome your covenant of peace. We pray:

We are your people:
be with those who will receive your promise in baptism at Easter. We pray:

You honor those who choose to serve:
help us to be true followers of your servant Son. We pray:

We know that we must die so that we may truly live:
strengthen all who suffer in mind or body [especially N.]. We pray:

You draw all people to yourself:
bring us out of our slavery to possessions and away from the desire for wealth. We pray:

[Here other intercessions may be offered.]

Lord God, show us the way of obedience through patient endurance and the way of glory through the law written in our hearts. Hear our prayers and come to our aid. We pray through Christ our Lord.

SUNDAY OF THE PASSION B
PALM SUNDAY B

Our Lord comes to us humbly, riding a donkey and proclaiming a message of peace. Let us pray, saying: Lord, hear our prayer.

That Christians hear and share the word of God as true disciples, we pray:

That all the ends of the earth receive the words of the king of peace, we pray:

That all leaders, of church and of state, prefer humble service to empty power, we pray:

That those who see the cross starkly revealed in their lives draw strength from the name above every other name, we pray:

That we who hope to greet Jesus when he comes again be ready and joyful, we pray:

[Here other intercessions may be offered.]

God our creator, you show your sons and daughters the way to freedom through the gentle obedience of your Son Jesus Christ. Grant our petitions as we seek to follow him. We pray in his name, Christ the Lord.

HOLY THURSDAY B
MAUNDY THURSDAY B

We gather as the household of God, apostles, prophets, martyrs, servants, to pray for the church and all humankind, saying: Come, Lord Jesus.

For refugees, for the homeless, and for all who have nowhere to lay their head, we pray:

For those unable to eat at the Lord's Table or at any other table we pray:

For the body of Christ fractured in a world of violence and war we pray:

For those who betray, and for those whom they betray, we pray:

For all in any need [especially N.], we pray:

For ourselves, who gather to celebrate the Lord's passover in the bread we eat and the cup we drink, we pray:

[Here other intercessions may be offered.]

Almighty God, we recall the wonders you worked for our ancestors, and we marvel at the love shown us by your Son. Hear us as we pray in the name of your Son, Jesus Christ.

EASTER VIGIL B

Our Lord lives, for death has no more power over him. And so we, God's holy church, proclaim the resurrection, saying: Christ is risen! Amen, Alleluia!

Created in the image and likeness of God, we pray to see God's image in one another. May our lives proclaim:

Tested in our faith and strengthened by God's love, we pray for open hearts, that we may live to proclaim:

Liberated from sin and death by water and Spirit, we pray for those who do not share our hope, that they may proclaim:

Sharing in the joy of those baptized this night, we pray for their growth unto the full stature of Christ, that they may proclaim:

Joining with those who share in the passion of Christ through illness, famine, war, temptation, and trial [especially N.], we pray for their courage and strength, that those who suffer may proclaim:

[Here other intercessions may be offered.]

United in our hope that we and all who die will live again, we pray for family and friends who have died [especially N.], proclaiming:

O true God, who has glorified your Son Jesus Christ as the pledge of our freedom from sin and death, receive our praise and prayer through Christ our Lord, the great Amen and our Alleluia, now and forever.

EASTER DAY B
THE RESURRECTION OF OUR LORD B

Alleluia! What was dead shall live; what was dark shall shine; what was forgotten shall be remembered, for the Lord is risen and walks among us. Let us confidently bring before God the needs of all our world, asking God for renewal, saying: Christ is risen, Christ is risen indeed.

God of life, in gratitude and great joy we laud you for the gifts of Christ's resurrection. On this day give us hope, for Christ is risen:

On this feast day which brings joy to all Christian believers, may we commit ourselves to work toward the unity of the church, that Christ's body may be one, for Christ is risen:

Honoring the gift of Christ's risen body, may we rise to serve all those whose needs keep them from seeing themselves as the image of God; for Christ is risen:

For all who have need of the gift of Easter; for all who journey from illness to health, from despair to hope, from grief to consolation, from loneliness to love; [for N.;] for all our brothers and sisters, that death may have no more power over us, for Christ is risen:

For all who suffer and all who mourn, that today the Lord God will wipe away all tears, for Christ is risen:

May we have the persistent faith of Mary Magdalene and the surprised belief of Peter and John. May we long to be God's sign of life in our world, for Christ is risen:

[Here other intercessions may be offered.]

May we be one in faith with all who have died in Christ, for our life is hid with Christ in God; for Christ is risen:

God of life, we thank you for the mystery planted in us, the paradox of life from death and community from scattered disciples. We praise you for the dying which saves us from death and for the rising which brings us life. We pray, as we live, through Jesus the risen one, in the power of the Holy Spirit, now and forever.

SECOND SUNDAY OF EASTER B

On this day we praise our God for the dying which destroyed our death, and we pray for our world in need of life, saying: Lord, have mercy.

The Lord calls us to examine the wounded hands and feet of the risen one and to know the depth of his love for us. Let us approach Christ in faith and share the good news with all we meet. For this let us pray to the Lord:

The apostles received the Holy Spirit and the grace to lighten the burdens of one another's sin. May the church be faithful to this gift. May all the baptized live with abundant compassion for all, especially for those shut out from the society. For this let us pray to the Lord.

Christ calls us blest who not having seen, yet believe. May more and more of God's people and all the created order become a sign of the resurrection in the world, and may our faith give courage to the doubting. For this let us pray to the Lord.

We are strengthened by Christ's resurrection to share the power of the Spirit with all the suffering. We pray for all in any need [especially N.]. May the power of Christ's resurrection give life to all who have little reason to hope. For this let us pray to the Lord.

May that morning star which never sets, Christ our light, find us burning with charity until the world is enlightened with love. For this let us pray to the Lord.

[Here other intercessions may be offered.]

Eternally creative God, give us the faith and courage to recreate the world in your image. We ask this in the name of the risen one, Jesus our Lord and Savior.

Christ, the stone which the builders rejected, God has made the corner-stone of a new community. In that name by which we are founded, let us draw near in confidence, saying: Lord, have mercy.

The risen Christ opened the minds of the disciples to understand the scriptures. May the church find in the scriptures healing, mission, and good news for all. For this let us pray to the Lord.

Christ showed wounded hands and feet to his unbelieving apostles. May we see the risen one in all the wounded of our world. For this let us pray to the Lord.

Christ our cornerstone intercedes for us before God. Let us and all in authority heed God's call for justice in the church, in our community, and in the nation. For this let us pray to the Lord.

We are saved by a God who is light, in whom there is no darkness at all. Let us beg for God's light in those places which seem darkest. Let us ask that God enlighten all who inflict darkness on others. Let us ask that God shine on those who are victims of evil [especially N.]. For this let us pray to the Lord.

In the power of Christ's name we are healed. Let us recall all who need healing [especially N.] and all in the healing professions. For them let us pray to the Lord.

[Here other intercessions may be offered.]

Loving God, you have glorified your Son Jesus and given him the name by which we are saved. Give us the courage to act in his name. Accept our praise, offered in his name, for we offer this prayer through and with and in Jesus, your Son and our Savior.

FOURTH SUNDAY OF EASTER B

Consoled by the knowledge that the Good Shepherd gives his life for us, let us pray for the needs of our community, our church, and our world, saying: Lord, have mercy.

The earliest Christian community held all things in common, and no one was in need. May we recommit ourselves to hold the goods of this world in common and to work to eliminate hunger and homelessness. For this let us pray to the Lord.

When we share with one another, we make a new world. May we build a new community on earth which knows God as home. For this let us pray to the Lord.

Following the example of the shepherd who searched for the lost sheep, let us seek out the lost in our community and welcome them in our midst. For this let us pray to the Lord.

Conscious of the Good Shepherd's voice, may we speak God's words of reconciliation and peace to all we meet, and may all in governmental authority receive the joyful message of peace. For this let us pray to the Lord.

We are called to give up our lives for others. Let us praise God for all in serving professions who work at low pay for the welfare of others. May we give our lives to those in our care. For this let us pray to the Lord.

[Here other intercessions may be offered.]

God, in you we live and move and have our being. You seek us before we know your name, and you give us joy in your life. Accept our prayer of joy in being found and forgiven and loved by you, for we pray in the name of Christ your Son and in the joy of the Holy Spirit.

Let us join through prayer with everything that lives. Let us acknowledge to God the one life we share, saying: O God, who makes us one, hear our prayer.

O God, your Holy Spirit is alive in all the earth. Your Spirit that moved and shaped land and sea, trees and beasts still moves and shapes us into creation. Through Christ we know your one Holy Spirit, for you are God of all. That all the world may know your Spirit, we pray: O God, who makes us one,

Open your world before our eyes, so that we see far and near. Show us newly what lives around us, over and behind and within. Give us the mind of Christ. O God, who makes us one,

Bring us to one another, that we may hear and understand each other. Bring trust and sympathy between the peoples of the world. Make all nations one household with many rooms. O God, who makes us one,

Heal us who are sick [especially N.]. Cheer us who are guilty. Love us who are alone. Join us who are distant. Call all the world to yourself. O God, who makes us one,

Enliven the church with the Spirit of Christ. Through us give your loving Spirit to a world in need of comfort. Make our many gifts one offering for the world. O God, who makes us one,

[Here other intercessions may be offered.]

O God, keep our minds inside your love, for we are many parts and need to be one. We beg for this unity which only your Spirit can give, through Christ our Lord.

SIXTH SUNDAY OF EASTER B

God gives what is good. Let us pray that this goodness of God flow through us into all the world, saying: O God, giver of love, hear our prayer.

O God, your love is in motion. We praise the strength of your love. Where there is hunger, raise up your love. Where there is hurt and persecution, empower your love. Where there are false prophets, proclaim your love. Where there are lies, speak your love. O God, giver of love,

Where nations are angry and plot harm against one another, bring your love. Where governments lie and deceive, bring your love. Where powers cripple and destroy what you have made, bring your love. O God, giver of love,

Where the churches alienate one another, bring your love. Where our fears keep us from offering Christ to all the needy peoples, bring your love. When this assembly is marked by division and jealousy, bring your love. O God, giver of love,

O Lord, increase our affection. Increase our compassion. Increase our joy. Show us those we do not see. [Especially we pray for N..] Magnify our love. O God, giver of love,

[Here other intercessions may be offered.]

O God, we thank you for the power of divine love and for the presence of your love in one another. Guide us all finally into that greatest love who is Christ our Lord.

ASCENSION DAY B

On this day of the ascension of Christ, let us pray with amazement, wonder, awe, astonishment. Joining Christ who intercedes for all the world before God, let us offer our prayers to God, saying: O God of wonder, hear our prayer.

O God, we stand amazed; for Christ ascended from the earth in order to be everywhere at once. We are in awe; for in leaving, Jesus has not left us alone. We thank you, O God, for the life of your Son. Turn our eyes continually to see, to gaze with wonder at your miraculous ways. O God of wonder,

Turn the eyes of ordinary people, young and old, poor and rich, to see signs of Jesus. Show us everywhere the signs of Jesus, who is raised up and giving freedom and working power and justice. O God of wonder,

Turn the eyes of your church to see the poor places in which Christ now dwells. Help us to see the body of Christ, wounded and yet bright with the light of the Spirit. O God of wonder,

Turn the eyes of the leaders of nations to envision a new world in which peace and harmony reign. Turn the eyes of all in power to see the oppressed and the needy. For all who live by your inner sight, we give thanks. For more such people to lead the peoples, we pray. O God of wonder,

Turn the eyes of all gathered here beyond this place. Help us to look toward our glorified Lord, and then to look back anew. O God of wonder,

[Here other intercessions may be offered.]

O God, keep us in the spirit of amazement. Keep us believing when we cannot see; keep us hoping while we wait; keep us looking for your presence. Fix our eyes on the glorious one who ascended to intercede, who will come in greatest glory, Jesus Christ our Lord.

SEVENTH SUNDAY OF EASTER B

Today we thank God that the Christ who ascended is with us, visible in the lives of the people. Let us pray for all these people, and for the life about us, saying: O God, holding the world with love, have mercy on us.

O God, in the resurrection and ascension of your Son, you have drawn us nearer to yourself. Together with your Son may we be together also with all the people of the world. O God, holding the world with love,

Circle all your nations, towns, villages, tribes and countrysides with your love. Encircle all people with your great arms. Encircle all lands with your Son's marks of mercy. O God, holding the world with love,

Transform your church with love. Transform people and communities, groups and governments. Cast out fear with love. Turn us over and around by the Spirit of your Son. O God, holding the world with love,

Center all the scattered, and call them together with your love. Hold us together, or we will be lost. Awake us, or we will fall asleep in dangerous places. For the lost and helpless [especially N.], we pray. O God, holding the world with love,

Fill all the places of the world with your great love. Give us the joy of the spirit of Jesus. Make us glad in this sad world. O God, holding the world with love,

[Here other intercessions may be offered.]

O God of mercy, we have your promise that we are loved. Hear our prayers for all the world, hungering for your love, the love of your Son without end.

PENTECOST SUNDAY B
DAY OF PENTECOST B

*In the peace of the risen Christ let us offer our prayers to the Lord,
saying: Hear us, Lord. Alleluia!*

The Spirit of peace has been breathed on the church. May the
church inspire peace throughout the world. And to this let us
say:

Our land has completed the passover from winter into spring.
May the earth be restored to the freshness of creation. And to
this let us say:

The Lord has appeared on Sinai amid fire and wind. May all
people, Jew and Gentile together, climb the holy mountain and
see the face of God. And to this let us say:

The confusion of Babel has been undone with the gifts of Pentecost. May our community mature in wisdom as we come to
understand the language of the Spirit. And to this let us say:

Our week of weeks is accomplished. Our Fifty Days are complete. May all of us, both the living and the dead, be raised into
the splendor of endless Easter. May we hold before God's life
all in need [especially N.]. And to this let us say:

[Here other intercessions may be offered.]

*Creator God, our lenten ashes have become life-giving fire. We are
whole and new again. Help us, like the disciples in Jerusalem, to spill
out into the streets to proclaim your wonderful works. This we ask
through Christ our Lord.*

TRINITY SUNDAY B

Inspired by the Spirit, we now offer our Sunday prayers to God in the name of Jesus Christ, saying: Lord, have mercy.

For the fulfillment of the mission of the church, let us pray to the Lord.

For the liberation of the children of God from the bondage of fear, let us pray to the Lord.

For the consolation of all those who struggle with doubts or disbelief, let us pray to the Lord.

For renewed witness to the gospel among Christian people in positions of public trust, let us pray to the Lord.

For our assembly as we hand on the faith of our ancestors from one generation to another, let us pray to the Lord.

For the power to live out the promises of our baptism, let us pray to the Lord.

For all the sick and the suffering, the lonely and the dying [especially N.], let us pray to the Lord.

[Here other intercessions may be offered.]

In the communion of the Holy Spirit, with Mary, the mother of the Son of God, [with N.] and with all the saints in light, let us commend our lives and the lives of one another to the Lord.

Almighty God, with tender love we call you our Abba. Answer the prayers of your children gathered here, for we rely on you and have confidence in you. We ask this through Christ our Lord, in the unity of the Holy Spirit, now and forever.

THE BODY AND BLOOD OF CHRIST B

Sealed in the blood of Christ, the new covenant forms us into a holy people. Let us pray together as God's chosen ones, praying: Lord, hear our prayer.

For the church, washed in the blood of the Lord, renewed by the blood of martyrs, and nourished by the body and blood of Christ, let us pray to the Lord.

For those who serve among Christ's body, the church, and for those who work for the public good, let us pray to the Lord.

For those who hunger and thirst for justice, and for all who work for peace, let us pray to the Lord.

For the poor and the despised, for the afflicted and ill, [especially N.,] and for servants of charity, care, and healing, let us pray to the Lord.

For the safety of travelers by land, sea, or air, and for those who guide and direct them, let us pray to the Lord.

For those who till the soil, and for an abundance of the fruits of their labors, let us pray to the Lord.

[Here other intercessions may be offered.]

As you have served us, O God, and nourished us with eucharistic gifts, so may we be bread broken and wine poured out for the life of all your people. We pray this in the name of Christ, the Mediator of the new covenant, living and reigning with you and the Spirit, one God, forever and ever.

NINTH SUNDAY IN ORDINARY TIME B
PROPER 4 B
SECOND SUNDAY AFTER PENTECOST B

In confidence we offer our prayers to the Lord, saying: Lord, have mercy.

In peace let us pray to the Lord.

That the church may shine with the glory of the face of Christ, let us pray to the Lord.

That the harvests of summer be justly distributed among the hungry, let us pray to the Lord.

That the laws and customs of our society be observed with charity and good will, let us pray to the Lord.

That all those graduating from school may continue to grow in knowledge and wisdom, let us pray to the Lord.

That all of us gathered here may have recreation and refreshment this Sunday and every Sunday, let us pray to the Lord.

That each sabbath bring us closer to the health and wholesomeness of God's reign, let us pray to the Lord.

That all the sick may be healed [especially N.], let us pray to the Lord.

[Here other intercessions may be offered.]

In the communion of the Holy Spirit, with the blessed virgin Mary, [with N.] and with all the saints in light, let us commend our lives and the lives of one another to the Lord.

Loving God, we carry in our own bodies the dying of your Son. Have pity on us, and answer our prayers. This we ask through Christ our Lord.

TENTH SUNDAY IN ORDINARY TIME B
PROPER 5 B
THIRD SUNDAY AFTER PENTECOST B

In confidence we offer our Sunday prayers to the Lord, saying: Lord, have mercy.

That the church may always fix its gaze on the life that lasts forever, let us pray to the Lord.

That all the children of Adam and Eve may be rescued from ignorance, disobedience, and death, let us pray to the Lord.

That those who strive to build God's kingdom may enjoy the understanding of their families, let us pray to the Lord.

That we may be filled with the power to amend our lives and to seek forgiveness from those we wrong, let us pray to the Lord.

That our church may remain bound together in fidelity and compassion, let us pray to the Lord.

That all those who gather around this table may find trustworthy brothers and sisters, let us pray to the Lord.

That all the sick and suffering [especially N.] may be healed, let us pray to the Lord.

[Here other intercessions may be offered.]

In the communion of the Holy Spirit, with Mary, the mother of God, [with N.] and with all the saints, let us commend our lives and the lives of one another to the Lord.

God of loving-kindness, you have ordered all things for our benefit. Listen to our prayers and answer them with blessings. This we ask through Christ our Lord.

ELEVENTH SUNDAY IN ORDINARY TIME B
PROPER 6 B
FOURTH SUNDAY AFTER PENTECOST B

In the presence of our creative God who calls us to a growth that will transform and support us, let us come together and present our needs, saying: O God, hear our prayer.

That all people of every race may find a dwelling place of welcome and nourishment with us, we pray:

That as the mustard seed, the smallest of all earth's seeds, grows into the largest of shrubs, so may God's reign grow in us, we pray:

That as we plant the seeds of the kingdom, we may sow generously, from a full heart, we pray:

That as seeds require time to grow, we may continue to water and nourish God's word, confident that in time it will take root, growing strong as an elm, giving life and shelter to others, we pray:

That the homeless may find a dwelling place of acceptance and care within the church, we pray:

[Here other intercessions may be offered.]

For those who have died, leaving these tents to enter the house you have built in heaven [especially N.], we pray:

Nurturing God, gather us as the seeds of your mysterious life. Teach us to sense deeply your presence with us as we grow strong in love and service. May we be shelter for all in need. We ask this through Jesus Christ who is your fullness with us.

TWELFTH SUNDAY IN ORDINARY TIME B
PROPER 7 B
FIFTH SUNDAY AFTER PENTECOST B

As we find ourselves in a storm-tossed world, let us gather our needs and concerns to call upon our God, saying: O God, hear our prayer.

As the raging storm compelled the apostles to wake your Son, help us, O God, to weather the squalls that wake us to your presence. We pray:

As your Son bound the fury of the sea with his word, teach us to bind our science and technology with human dignity. We pray:

As Christ Jesus calmed the storm for the disciples' journey, calm whatever storms our travelers encounter and bring them safely home. We pray:

As Jesus once stilled the waves which buffeted the boat, quiet the rifts in our lives and in the lives of all for whom we pray [especially N.]. We pray:

As young parents marvel at the birth of their child, grant us ever to marvel at our new life in Christ. We pray:

As children delight in the world through the encouragement of their parents, help us to encourage one another to give thanks and praise to you for the wonders of creation. We pray:

[Here other intercessions may be offered.]

Caring God, we thank you for being with us through the fury and the calm of our life's voyage, revealing your care to us and drawing us to new life. May we live, as we pray, in the protection of Christ our Lord.

THIRTEENTH SUNDAY IN ORDINARY TIME B
PROPER 8 B
SIXTH SUNDAY AFTER PENTECOST B

We gather as creatures fashioned by the life-giving hand of God. Let us open our hearts to this creative and compassionate touch as we pray, saying: O God, hear our prayer.

You fashioned a world abundant with life and life-giving creatures. Inspire us to fashion with you a world that promotes fullness of life for all peoples. For this we pray:

As Jesus compassionately responded to Jairus' need, help us to heed the hungry, the homeless, the unemployed, and the elderly in our midst. For this we pray:

As the earth nourishes and sustains us, may we nourish and sustain one another in justice and peace. We pray:

Help us to release our tight-fisted grasp on the things of this world, and may we never contribute to the pain and hunger of our brothers and sisters. We pray:

We are made in your image, O God; help us to hold up each other as mirrors of your life. We pray:

We hover in anticipation of your healing presence, generous God. We pray for all who are ill [especially N.]. Empower us all to wait and trust. We pray:

[Here other intercessions may be offered.]

Gracious God, often we resist your gentle and compassionate hand in our lives. Open our hearts to your life-giving touch, and may we trust the growth of your dominion in the world. We ask this through Jesus Christ, who is our life and our hope.

FOURTEENTH SUNDAY IN ORDINARY TIME B
PROPER 9 B
SEVENTH SUNDAY AFTER PENTECOST B

As people of faith, we are called to be prophets. Let us open our hearts and call upon our God, saying: O God, hear our prayer.

That our wounded and numbed hearts may be given hope, and that in our weakness we may be empowered by God's guiding hand, let us pray, saying:

That each of us may open the door to the one who knocks, let us pray, saying:

That as the sea transforms rock to sand, God may transform our weakness to strength, let us pray, saying:

That we may be instrumental in alleviating the pains of oppression by reaching out to the poor, the homeless, and the neglected, let us pray, saying:

That we and all in the church may recognize the prophets in our own midst, let us pray, saying:

That all in any need [especially N.] may receive God's mercy, let us pray, saying:

[Here other intercessions may be offered.]

Compassionate God, we come to you, aware that the prophet within each of us shrinks from your call. Give us the courage to speak and live the word of your Son, in whose name we pray.

FIFTEENTH SUNDAY IN ORDINARY TIME B
PROPER 10 B
EIGHTH SUNDAY AFTER PENTECOST B

As one people called by God, let us pray, saying: Hear us, good Lord.

We say we are not prophets, Lord, nor the children of prophets; yet we are your witnesses. That we may be faithful witnesses, we pray:

You have called us and joined us into one body, the church, to hear the cries of the world and to read the signs of our time, to speak where silence needs breaking, to comfort when terror threatens, to support where courage falters, to risk when fear controls. That you may work in us the prophet's vision and power, we pray:

The world waits in need, O God. When peace seems within grasp, it somehow slips away. When crops in one nation flourish, famine reigns in another. When technology masters a new frontier, old problems rise to plague it. When chemicals serve our human needs, the environment suffers pollution. While medicines cure the gravest ills, diseases still destroy us. That you will help us in our need, we pray:

Help us to understand the complexity of life. Help us to learn from the forces we seek to overcome. Help us trust you. That you will bring our waiting to an end, we pray:

Eternal God, you send us on a journey, as you have sent others before us, to anoint, to heal, to comfort, to cast out demons. For each person in need this day, we pray for the gentle touch of another's caring hand. [Especially we pray for N..] Lavish the riches of your grace upon them, as you have promised. To you, O Healer, we pray:

[Here other intercessions may be offered.]

Creator of the world, sustainer of the church, hear our prayers, accept the praise and thanks of our worship, and grant us that which makes us whole, through Jesus Christ our Lord.

SIXTEENTH SUNDAY IN ORDINARY TIME B
PROPER 11 B
NINTH SUNDAY AFTER PENTECOST B

In Jesus' name we offer our prayers to God, who was and is and is to come, saying: Lord, hear our prayer.

For a world filled with computers and playgrounds, art museums and mud huts, jet planes and ox carts, green fields and barren deserts, we beg for your mercy. For a world filled with the sophisticated and the simple, the fruitful and the withered, the whole and the maimed, we beg for your mercy. For the joy that comes from respecting how each contributes to the whole, let us pray to the Lord.

For the church filled with teachers and dock workers, the disabled and the unemployed, the dying and the infants, the homemakers and the artists, we beg for your mercy. For a church filled with the sophisticated and the simple, the fruitful and the withered, the whole and the maimed, we beg for your mercy. For the hope that comes from respecting how each contributes to the whole, let us pray to the Lord.

For people whose lives are filled with anxiety and despair, happiness and health, pain and trouble, wonder and challenge, honest or bitter isolation, we beg for your mercy. For human lives filled with the sophisticated and the simple, the fruitful and the withered, the whole and the maimed, we beg for your mercy. [Especially for N. we pray.] For the peace that comes from respecting how each contributes to the whole, let us pray to the Lord.

[Here other intercessions may be offered.]

Fill us, almighty God, with joy, hope and peace. Grant that hostilities may cease, strangers become friends, and all humanity discover the world as your household. We pray this through Jesus Christ our Lord, who reigns in unity with you and the Holy Spirit, now and forever.

SEVENTEENTH SUNDAY IN ORDINARY TIME B
PROPER 12 B
TENTH SUNDAY AFTER PENTECOST B

Because we have been fed and called, and our lives joined forever in Christ, we unite our voices in prayer, saying: Lord, have mercy.

For the wisdom to know the difference between the word of God and our own words, let us pray to the Lord.

For the world, for all nations, for each country's leaders and people, that peace and cooperation will be our common goal, let us pray to the Lord.

For the church, that it may be a faithful witness, and that maintaining unity in the bond of peace, we may know what it means to have one Lord, one faith, and one baptism, let us pray to the Lord.

For all people in need, that each person's hunger may be satisfied, each person's pain relieved; [especially for N.;] and for ourselves, let us pray to the Lord.

For our own community and families, that we may know God's presence and embody God's love, let us pray to the Lord.

[Here other intercessions may be offered.]

Almighty God, lost in the darkness we search for light; surrounded by our created wastes, we seek a promised land; threatened by war, we break the bonds that make for peace. Help us to find our light, our land, and our peace in you, now and forever.

EIGHTEENTH SUNDAY IN ORDINARY TIME B
PROPER 13 B
ELEVENTH SUNDAY AFTER PENTECOST B

Gathered in the name of Jesus, united by the power of the Holy Spirit let us pray, saying: O Lord, bread of life, have mercy upon us.

You are the bread of life, O God. You feed us with manna, and you satisfy our needs with your word. For the food that never perishes, we thank you. Gather us up with all your needy people, that none may be lost. O Lord, bread of life,

You call us, O God, to be renewed, to put on a new nature, to conform our lives to your will. Form the church into a source of life which feeds a needy world. O Lord, true bread from heaven,

In a hungry world, O God, we do not know how to feed one another. Hear the cries of the poor. Strengthen us to answer their need, to dry the tears of those who mourn, to care for the children, to preserve the land, to honor all your people. [Especially we pray for N..] O Lord, source of manna in the wilderness,

We long to embrace you, O God. We rejoice in your invitation to life. Urge us gently unto the arms of our sisters and brothers, that we may find you there. O Lord, font of life,

[Here other intercessions may be offered.]

All these things we have spoken, and those which we name in the silence of our hearts, we pray in the name of Jesus Christ our Lord who with you and the Holy Spirit are one God, forever and ever.

NINETEENTH SUNDAY IN ORDINARY TIME B
PROPER 14 B
TWELFTH SUNDAY AFTER PENTECOST B

Grateful for the gifts we have already been given, we now bring our hopes and needs into the presence of our provident God, saying: Lord, in your mercy, hear our prayer.

We pray for our church. As Christians, may we all hunger for the bread of life that we may be transformed into the body of Christ. Lord, in your mercy,

We pray for bishops, all the clergy, deacons, and all who minister in the church. May they break the bread of life and proclaim the living word for our world; may we all open our lives to receive the gifts they offer. Lord, in your mercy,

We pray for our Jewish brothers and sisters. Like the Israelites in the desert, may they be nourished as they journey in faith through life; may we accompany them in a spirit of repentance and compassion. Lord, in your mercy,

We pray for government leaders. May they work for social justice rather than power; may we support them in their efforts. Lord, in your mercy,

We pray for those who are hungry in our world. May they have their needs satisfied; may we sacrifice some of what we have to feed the poor. Lord, in your mercy,

[Here other intercessions may be offered.]

We pray for those who have recently died [especially N.]. May they share in the heavenly banquet; may we long to be guests with them at God's holy table. Lord, in your mercy,

All generous God, hear these prayers made in faith and hope. Bring us all one day to sit with you at the banquet you have prepared for those who love you. We make this prayer in the name of Jesus who reigns with you in the power of the Holy Spirit, now and forever.

TWENTIETH SUNDAY IN ORDINARY TIME B
PROPER 15 B
THIRTEENTH SUNDAY AFTER PENTECOST B

As a mother setting food before her hungry children, God satisfies our most basic needs and our deepest longings. Confident that we have a solicitous God, we pray now for our church and our world, saying: Lord, hear our prayer.

Because we need to be nourished by your word and sacrament, we pray for our church that we might both be willing to eat of your food and drink of your wine and in turn be food and drink for one another. In faith we pray to you, O God.

Because we live in evil days and often act like fools, we pray that our world may not continue in ignorance but discern what is truly good and just. In faith we pray to you, O God.

Because we are prone to be competitive and unconcerned about one another, we pray for all political leaders that we might find in them examples of generous service and self-forgetfulness. In faith we pray to you, O God.

Because there are so many poor and hungry people in our world, we pray that we may be generous in giving, compassionate in serving, and sensitive in understanding the needs of others. In faith we pray to you, O God.

Because our world is pervaded by a spirit of skepticism and mistrust, we pray for unbelievers that they may find us to be confident people who know that God does indeed have a plan for our world. In faith we pray to you, O God.

[Here other intercessions may be offered.]

Because we have often been nourished and supported by many relatives and friends who have preceded us in death, we pray that they may live in peace and be mindful of us who still struggle to live the Christian life. In faith we pray to you, O God.

All loving God, the source of all good gifts, we praise and thank you for your provident care. Hear the prayers we have made in faith. As a gracious mother, feed us with the bread of life so we might abide with you forever. We make this prayer as always through Jesus Christ our Lord.

TWENTY-FIRST SUNDAY IN ORDINARY TIME B
PROPER 16 B
FOURTEENTH SUNDAY AFTER PENTECOST B

Our God is indeed the God of our holy ancestors, faithful to all the promises made to our people. Wanting to serve our God and trusting that we will be protected in time of trial and preserved in time of evil, we bring our needs and longings into the divine presence, saying: Lord, hear our prayer.

That you may bless our church and raise up in our midst holy men and women to proclaim your gospel, celebrate your sacraments, and minister to those who long for your saving help, we pray to you, good and faithful God.

That you may bless our world and deliver it into the hands of leaders who trust in your providence, serve others in your name, and work to establish a reign of justice and peace, we pray to you, good and faithful God.

That you may bless our homes so they may be free from hatred, filled with love, and hospitable to those who are lonely, isolated, sick, or poor, we pray to you, good and faithful God.

That you may bless husbands and wives so that in their love for one another they mirror the love that Christ has for the church, we pray to you, good and faithful God.

That you may bless those who share your life with others--physicians who seek to bring health where there is sickness, educators to seek to bring wisdom where there is ignorance, and artists who seek to bring beauty where there is squalor--we pray to you, good and faithful God.

[Here other intercessions may be offered.]

That you may bless those who have gone before us in faith that they may abide in peace and pray for us who continue on life's journey, we pray to you, good and faithful God.

All good and merciful God, you indeed are faithful to the covenant you have made with your people. May you hear our prayers as we prepare to enter into a renewal of that covenant by celebrating the mystery of your Son's death and resurrection. We make this prayer through him, Jesus Christ the Lord, who lives and reigns with you in the power of the Holy Spirit, one God, forever and ever.

TWENTY-SECOND SUNDAY IN ORDINARY TIME B
PROPER 17 B
FIFTEENTH SUNDAY AFTER PENTECOST B

Knowing that God hears our prayers when they are made in sincerity and humility, we pray for our church and our world in our time of need, saying: Hear us, good Lord.

Those who live justly will live in the presence of God. We pray for our church that its structures promote justice, its laws foster integrity of heart, and its ministry model compassion. To you we pray, O gracious God:

Those who live justly will live in the presence of God. We pray for our world that we will be freed from that hypocrisy which lurks in our hearts, when we seek the assurance of external observance without the commitment of faith. To you we pray, O gracious God:

Those who live justly will live in the presence of God. We pray for those who make and enforce laws that they may challenge us in our waywardness and be compassionate toward our weakness. To you we pray, O gracious God:

Those who live justly will live in the presence of God. We pray for those who teach the word of God that they may embrace the justice of God in their own hearts as they call us into the life of God. To you we pray, O gracious God:

Those who live justly will live in the presence of God. We pray that we may be delivered from all the wicked designs in the deep recesses of our hearts and so live justly with God and one another. To you we pray, O gracious God:

[Here other intercessions may be offered.]

Those who live justly will live in the presence of God. We pray for those who have died that they may dwell with the saints and remember us who struggle to live in justice and peace. To you we pray, O gracious God:

All just and merciful God, you know our wants, and you know our true needs. May you attend to our prayers, direct our hearts in the way of justice and mercy, and enlighten our minds that we may know your holy will. We ask this through the just one, Jesus Christ, your servant and our Lord, who lives and reigns with you in the power of the Holy Spirit, our God, forever and ever.

TWENTY-THIRD SUNDAY IN ORDINARY TIME B
PROPER 18 B
SIXTEENTH SUNDAY AFTER PENTECOST B

God calls us today to be open to the word and to one another. Let us open ourselves to all the world in prayer, saying: Lord, have mercy.

For the church we pray. That we may bring God's word of life to all in silence, darkness, and despair, let us pray to the Lord.

For our congregation we pray. That we may grow into the mystery of God's life among and in us, let us pray to the Lord.

For the world we pray. That nations will come to cooperate for the health and well-being of all, let us pray to the Lord.

For our community we pray. That hospitals and nursing homes may be equipped to deal with our sick and dying, let us pray to the Lord.

For all in the healing professions we pray. That those who search for cures and those who attend the sick may be strengthened for their tasks, let us pray to the Lord.

For the sick and dying we pray. That [N. and] all who have asked for our prayers may know the healing power of God, and that those who die today may not die alone, let us pray to the Lord.

[Here other intercessions may be offered.]

For all mourners we pray. That all who grieve the coming of death may come to know life in the mercy of God, let us pray to the Lord.

Into your mercy, O God, we commend all the needy world, trusting in your almighty power, through your Son, Jesus Christ our Lord.

TWENTY-FOURTH SUNDAY IN ORDINARY TIME B
PROPER 19 B
SEVENTEENTH SUNDAY AFTER PENTECOST B

Jesus calls us to give up our lives for others. That we may have the faith to live as Jesus did, let us pray for all in need, saying: Send us your Spirit, O Lord.

O gracious God, you have given up your very self to save the world. That we may be empowered to give up ourselves for one another, we pray:

You have made your people equal and free in the baptism of your Son. That we may live joyfully in this new way, we pray:

You call us to take up our cross and follow the way of Christ. That we may serve one another and live in obedience to your word, we pray:

You show to us all the poor and the needy, all the homeless and the hungry. That we may lighten their load by taking it upon ourselves, we pray:

You give us enough that we may share with the needy. That we and all institutions of relief may be insistent in our care for others, we pray:

[Here other intercessions may be offered.]

You have surrounded us with saints of every time and place. That we may follow them as they followed Christ on the way to the cross, we pray:

Hear our prayers, O merciful God, and accept our praises. May the gospel of your cross give its miraculous life to all the world, through Christ our Lord.

TWENTY-FIFTH SUNDAY IN ORDINARY TIME B
PROPER 20 B
EIGHTEENTH SUNDAY AFTER PENTECOST B

Christ calls us to a life of peace and humility. Let us pray for strength to live this baptized life, saying: Lord, have mercy.

For all the baptized people of God, that having been called by our Lord we may gladly wait on those in need, let us pray to the Lord.

For all in authority in nation and church, that they may learn humility, let us pray to the Lord.

For all countries at war, that the peace of Christ may come among them, and for all who suffer the ravages of wartime, that they may find comfort and refuge, let us pray to the Lord.

For all who minister in this and in every Christian community, that they may find strength for their tasks, let us pray to the Lord.

For all children, that they may be fed and housed and may grow with self-confidence and joy, let us pray to the Lord.

For all in any need, the sick, the suffering, the oppressed; for those who serve others against their own will; and for all who have asked for our prayers [especially N.], let us pray to the Lord.

[Here other intercessions may be offered.]

For all the saints who have willingly served others, we praise our Servant God. That we may join them in a life of service, let us pray to the Lord.

Receive us, O God, as you received the child in Capernaum, for we yearn for your mercy, through your Son, Jesus Christ our Lord.

TWENTY-SIXTH SUNDAY IN ORDINARY TIME B
PROPER 21 B
NINETEENTH SUNDAY AFTER PENTECOST B

We have heard today of the cost of discipleship. That we may be empowered to bear the name of Christ, let us pray for ourselves and for the whole world, saying: Lord, hear our prayer.

The church of God is fragmented; we need the healing of the Holy Spirit. Let us pray for the church.

The world cries out for an increase of justice and for an end to war. Let us pray for the world.

Our country is striving for equality and a better life for all its citizens. Let us pray for our nation.

Our community seeks a better sense of its gifts and more wisdom into its problems. Let us pray for our community.

We know many people who are sick and suffering, who have public hurt or private pain. [We pray especially for N.] Let us pray for all in need.

Our lives have been enriched by the lives of all those like [N.,] Moses, the elders, and the disciples who have gone before us in the faith. Let us pray for grace to be disciples.

[Here other intercessions may be offered.]

We are thirsty, O merciful God; give us a cup of water to drink. Hear our prayers and answer our cries of need through your Son, Christ our Lord.

TWENTY-SEVENTH SUNDAY IN ORDINARY TIME B
PROPER 22 B
TWENTIETH SUNDAY AFTER PENTECOST B

Christ embraced humanity, sharing God's love with the poor, the downtrodden, and the weak. May our lives reflect that same concern as we turn to God with our needs, saying: Lord, have mercy.

May the relationships of church leaders provide examples of faithfulness and understanding to the communities they guide: for this we pray to the Lord.

May nations and states find in each other complimentarity and the shared visions of humanity, together overcoming any adversity or hatred: for this we pray to the Lord.

May those who suffer abuse, neglect, or senseless pain encounter God's loving presence in their lives, and may all who are in pain [especially N.] find mercy: for this we pray to the Lord.

May husbands and wives nurture the image of God in one another: for this we pray to the Lord.

May those who are lonely or in troubled marriages find comfort in the Christian community: for this we pray to the Lord.

[Here other intercessions may be offered.]

May all who have died [especially N.] rest in the presence of God, sharing in the eternal banquet: for this we pray to the Lord.

Gracious and merciful God, your faithfulness is timeless. Grant that our lives might reflect that same faithfulness which Jesus, your Son, shared with us, in whose name we pray.

TWENTY-EIGHTH SUNDAY IN ORDINARY TIME B
PROPER 23 B
TWENTY-FIRST SUNDAY AFTER PENTECOST B

Christ challenges our comforts and complacencies. Let us turn to him in our need, asking for God's intervention in our world, saying: Lord, hear our prayer.

For the victims of war, conflict, and violence throughout the world, that they might encounter justice and peace, participating in the reign of God, we pray to the Lord.

For churches and their leaders, that the dominion of God might be proclaimed in action as well as in word, we pray to the Lord.

For the lost, the lonely, the isolated, and the ill [especially N.], that they might receive blessings a hundredfold, leading to eternal life, we pray to the Lord.

For this community gathered in prayer, that we might gain riches by giving ours to others, we pray to the Lord.

For Christian communities, that the struggle to follow Christ will lead to life eternal, we pray to the Lord.

[Here other intercessions may be offered.]

God, source of life and fountain of mercy, all things are possible with you. Grant us a share in your eternal life. We ask this through Jesus Christ our Lord.

TWENTY-NINTH SUNDAY IN ORDINARY TIME B
PROPER 24 B
TWENTY-SECOND SUNDAY AFTER PENTECOST B

We are invited to serve the needs of all, but we require God's assistance. Let us turn our hearts to God, asking for help in our need, saying: Lord, have mercy.

That leaders of the church will freely serve the faithful, without preference to rank or authority, we pray to the Lord.

That among the peoples of the world service will take precedence over authority, we pray to the Lord.

That the many peoples of the world will serve the needs of others and will comfort the anxieties of all, we pray to the Lord.

That the victims of oppression, abuse, or neglect will discover the peace of God through others' assistance, prayer, and presence, we pray to the Lord.

That all who suffer [especially N.] will know the power of God, we pray to the Lord.

That the community gathered here will nourish others, sustained by the nourishment of the word and the table of the Lord, we pray to the Lord.

[Here other intercessions may be offered.]

God of justice, Lord of love, send your Spirit to dwell within us, sustaining our efforts of service; we ask this in Jesus' name, who lives forever and ever.

THIRTIETH SUNDAY IN ORDINARY TIME B
PROPER 25 B
TWENTY-THIRD SUNDAY AFTER PENTECOST B

Our faith is centered on Christ, who revealed to us the healing touch of God's justice and mercy. We now call on God to continue that same healing and justice in our lives and in our world, saying: Lord, have mercy.

May the leaders of governments see the needs of the oppressed and respond in justice. For this we pray:

May ministers continue Christ's mission of healing for all that is blind in their communities. For this we pray:

May those who are in need of healing [especially N.] find in Christ a source of strength in their struggles. For this we pray:

May those who cannot discover ways to be of service be challenged in their lives of faith. For this we pray:

[Here other intercessions may be offered.]

May those who have died [especially N.] live eternally in the presence of God, in whom all find comfort and peace. For this we pray:

Almighty God, we seek your face in our lives. Touch us with your Spirit of justice and healing, through Christ your Son, in whom we pray.

THIRTY-FIRST SUNDAY IN ORDINARY TIME B
PROPER 26 B
TWENTY-FOURTH SUNDAY AFTER PENTECOST B

The law that transforms the wasteland into a land of milk and honey is the law of love. Trusting in God's promise to lead us more deeply into that land, let us ask with confidence for all we need, saying: Teach us your ways, O God; hear us, good Lord.

We pray for the leaders of this country, that they may govern with justice and mercy, mindful of their responsibility to the world's poor. Teach us your ways, O God;

We pray for the church that, as a sign of your loving embrace, it may call all to share in your reign. Teach us your ways, O God:

We pray for ministers everywhere, that you may strengthen them in their desire to serve. Teach us your ways, O God;

We pray for this community of faith, that we may learn to love with all our hearts, our minds, our strength. Teach us your ways, O God;

We pray for the unloved of this world, for those who are widowed, orphaned, and friendless, for those who are homeless and alone, [for N.,] and for all who experience alienation, that you may touch them with your compassion. Teach us your ways, O God;

[Here other intercessions may be offered.]

We pray for all those who have died [especially N.], that they may find eternal life in your loving presence. Teach us your ways, O God;

Loving God, inscribe your words upon our hearts, that, carrying them with us out into the world, we may reveal your reign to all those we meet upon our way. We ask this through Jesus Christ, our guide and goal.

THIRTY-SECOND SUNDAY IN ORDINARY TIME B
PROPER 27 B
TWENTY-FIFTH SUNDAY AFTER PENTECOST B

For the widow and her son, the jar of flour did not go empty, nor did the jug of oil run dry. Through a year of drought, God provided for their needs until the rains came. Mindful of our own hunger and thirst, let us ask God to give us those blessings which will sustain us, saying: Give us this day our daily bread; Lord, hear our prayer.

We ask that you will send life-giving rain to the earth, that there may be bread for all nations. Give us this day our daily bread;

We ask that the leaders of this country will build for peace, not war, so that there can be a more equitable sharing of the world's resources. Give us this day our daily bread;

We ask that the church may continue to offer the bread of life to those who are hungry in spirit, that they may taste the richness of your consolation. Give us this day our daily bread;

We ask that this community of faith may be a sign of your loving generosity, always ready to give to those who have less and to welcome the strangers in our midst. Give us this day our daily bread;

We ask that you will hear the cries of the hungry, and that you will open our ears to their pleas. Give us this day our daily bread;

[Here other intercessions may be offered.]

Loving God, giver of life, nurture us in body and spirit so that, trusting in your mercy, we may generously respond to whatever you ask of us. We pray in the name of Jesus, your Son, who gave his life for our salvation.

THIRTY-THIRD SUNDAY IN ORDINARY TIME B
PROPER 28 B
TWENTY-SIXTH SUNDAY AFTER PENTECOST B

The images of cosmic disaster in today's readings fill us with fear, but also with hope. Terrifying as the signs may be, the time of Michael will bring life to those who have been faithful, just, and wise. Aware of the need for a new order, let us pray that God's reign will come in its fullness, saying: May your reign come; Lord, hear our prayer.

We pray for the leaders of this world, that, abandoning the terrible power of nuclear weapons, they may trust instead to ways of peace. May your reign come;

We pray for the church, that it may always be a sign of your loving presence and a sign of hope even in the darkest times. May your reign come;

We pray for victims of warfare and natural disasters [especially for the people of N.], that you may comfort them in their suffering. May your reign come;

We pray for all those who suffer from despair, especially young people, that you may give them the courage to build for the future. May your reign come;

We pray for this community of faith, that we may learn to respond to the signs of the times with wisdom and grace. May your reign come;

[Here other intercessions may be offered.]

Loving God, you know our hopes and fears even before we speak them; hear the prayers of your people. Help us in our struggle to stay alert that we may be ready for the hour of your coming. We ask this through Jesus, your Son.

TWENTY-SEVENTH SUNDAY AFTER PENTECOST B

With all our heart and all our mind, let us pray to the Lord, saying:
Lord, have mercy.

For the leaders of the nations, that they will know that they stand before the judgment of the God of peace, let us pray to the Lord.

For those in any tribulation, for the poor of the earth, for the hungry, for the victims of warfare and of governmental oppression, that their needs may be answered as they cleave in hope to the dawning justice of the God of peace, let us pray to the Lord.

For those who have asked for our prayers and for those whom we name in our hearts, for the sick among us, [for N.,] that they may be held in the healing mercy of the God of peace, let us pray to the Lord.

For the churches of God, that they may be gathered into visible unity in witness to the God of peace, let us pray to the Lord.

For this assembly, that we may be taught by the word of God and by the holy sacraments to anticipate the coming of the God of peace, let us pray to the Lord.

[Here other intercessions may be offered.]

O blessed God of peace, you raised our Lord Jesus Christ from the dead. Look now upon those in any need and upon the whole earth, and let the reign of Christ come soon, to judge the earth, to comfort those who mourn, to raise the dead, and to gather all your people into one, for you, O God, Father, Son, and Holy Spirit, live and reign forever and ever.

LAST SUNDAY, CHRIST THE KING B
PROPER 29 B
CHRIST THE KING B

On this the last Sunday of the liturgical year, we celebrate the feast of Christ the King. As we reflect on the meaning of Jesus' reign over our hearts, let us pray for ourselves and for the world, saying: May your reign come; Lord, hear our prayer.

We pray for all those in positions of power, that they may govern with wisdom and integrity, serving the needs of their people. May your reign come;

We pray for the church, the sign of your reign, that it may extend your welcome to people of every race and background. May your kingdom come;

We pray for Christians of every denomination, that together we may come to understand the royal priesthood you bestowed on us in baptism. May your dominion come;

We pray for all those whose commitment to truth brings them into conflict with earthly powers, that they may have the courage to endure. May your rule come;

We pray for this community of faith, that attentive to your word, we may always worship in spirit and truth. May your reign come;

[Here other intercessions may be offered.]

Loving God, you have taught us that the power of the heart is greater than the power of wealth and might. Hear us as we pray for the fulfillment of your reign. We ask this through Jesus our King; to him be glory and power forever.

138 *Last Sunday in Ordinary Time, Christ the King B*
   Proper 29 B
   Christ the King, Last Sunday after Pentecost B

SUNDAYS, MAJOR HOLY DAYS, AND SOLEMNITIES,

CYCLE C

FIRST SUNDAY OF ADVENT C

As the church worldwide celebrates the beginning of its New Year, let us turn our minds and hearts to the larger community of which we are a part, saying: Hear our prayer, O Lord, and grant us mercy.

For all peoples of every race, nation and disposition: May your love so embrace us all, that its power overcomes our conflicts, our defenses, and our fears. Quicken us to our true nature as your children that we may love one another. Hear our prayer, O Lord,

For all the churches of the world, Orthodox, Catholic, Protestant, and Pentecostal: May we grow together in our understanding of mission, that we may be strengthened in unity and united in acts of service. Call us to the one discipleship with its many gifts. Hear our prayer, O Lord,

For all Christian communities, young and growing in Africa, aging and changing in North America: Renew our vision and experience of Christian community as ever birthing, ever transforming, ever young and open to risk, ever old and full of wisdom. Hear our prayer, O Lord,

For those who live in fear and confusion: Whether they be stateless people in refugee camps, or settled people hidden behind high fences, give to the vulnerable strength, and to the secure vulnerability, that our human compassion for one another may end injustice and give our societies a human face. Hear our prayer, O Lord,

For this community, especially for those who suffer most, for the emotionally and physically ill, for the dying, for those who grieve: May we all, out of our own suffering, give comfort and support. Hear our prayer, O Lord,

For the larger community around us, especially for the newborn children, the homeless, and the imprisoned: May we create a world where shelter, food and medical care are available for all and where the law protects people for a better chance and better choices. Hear our prayer, O Lord,

[Here other intercessions may be offered.]

On this first day of the year, we gather up our prayers and offer them to you, O Lord, knowing full well that there are signs in the sun and moon and stars and in the common events of ordinary life that call us to attend to your coming. Prepare us for the time of trial and for your dominion, coming now and at the close of this age.

SECOND SUNDAY OF ADVENT C

Wherever we are, in the wilderness, the countryside, or the city, God, you are there. That our hearts may be stirred up in thanksgiving for the life you have given us, let us pray, saying: Lord, in your mercy, hear our prayer.

For the gifts of creation, for the sun that lights our day and the moon and stars that shelter the night: May our eyes be open to the beauty around us, the subtle changes in the sky, the delicate coating of soil from which breaks forth our food and flowers and in which animals make their home. Help us to protect and nurture your creation around us and ever proclaim its wonders. Lord, in our mercy,

For the church in every place: May we be ever mindful of the richness of the family of the church, the persons next to us in the pew, those in neighborhood churches, the national, international, and ecumenical church of every race, nation and economic circumstance. Let us give thanks for the web of friendship and trust that you give to those who are called the friends of Christ. Lord, in your mercy,

For those in authority: Let us pray for Christians who witness in places hostile to the gospel, and let us be thankful for our freedom to practice our faith. Let us pray for the leaders of nations that Christ may transform strangers into friends that all may see your salvation. Lord, in your mercy,

For this community in our joys and sorrows: Let us remember those who have gone before us, those who have sacrificed for us. Help us to look for what is below the obvious, and from this depth to reach out to others. Help us to know the joy that is mingled even with our utmost grief. Let us give thanks for this gathering of God's people and for the renewal of life we are given. Lord, in your mercy,

For those at greatest risk among us: Let us pray for those lonely, rejected, or oppressed, for the sick and those who struggle to regain their strength, for those among us with the longest memories to link us to the past, and for the newborn, in whose baptism our baptism is again renewed. Lord, in your mercy,

[Here other intercessions may be offered.]

Lord, gather up our prayers with those of all your people in every place, and as you prepare the way, making every valley filled and every mountain brought low in blessing and adoration, guide us to Christ our Lord.

THIRD SUNDAY OF ADVENT C

Let our hearts and minds be stirred as we pray to God for that peace so much greater than we can imagine, saying: Quicken your Spirit within us; O Lord, hear our prayer.

For peace in the world: May the wars on every continent cease, may nations be at rest, may refugees and survivors find a new home and the spirit to begin again. May wounds be healed, losses grieved, and honorable deeds remembered. May grace abound in all lands, and the lion and the lamb lie content. Quicken your Spirit within us;

For peace in the church: May we intensify our efforts of peace-making with the separated churches, that peace may prevail over conflict and we be reconciled in one family, exercising one baptism, one eucharist, and one common ministry in its many forms. Quicken your Spirit within us;

For this assembly: May we let go of our vested interests and inspired by your Spirit seek peace with one another. Help us give up the grievances we harbor within our families and communities and among our co-workers and friends. Help us build trust, the cornerstone of all reconciled relationships. Quicken your Spirit within us;

For peace where we live, work and recreate, and for peace within ourselves: May the noises in and around us diminish so that we can hear the sounds of the trees, the birds, the winds, and the rain. Give us space and time to hear ourselves, to feel our own feelings and express our own longings, knowing that the only one true longing is your longing for us. Quicken your Spirit within us;

For our young people: Let us provide space for them in our midst, and time to reassure them in their insecurities, encourage them in their hopes, and ever strengthen them in their gifts. Quicken your Spirit within us;

For the elderly and the infirm: We give thanks for the health and long life that many enjoy, and we pray for those who are overcome with suffering in body and spirit. Help us comfort one another and share with one another, knowing that whatever we ask for in prayer, those needs will be satisfied. Quicken your Spirit within us;

[Here other intercessions may be offered.]

O Lord, fill our minds and hearts with everything that is good and loving and worthy of thanksgiving and praise, everything that comes to us under the sign of your peace and in the name of Christ our Lord.

FOURTH SUNDAY OF ADVENT C

May our hearts leap for joy as we again assemble in prayer to await the Lord's coming. With Mary may our souls proclaim God's greatness as we say: Lord, in your mercy, hear our prayer.

Let us pray for the church: As the celebration of your incarnation draws near, we remember the many ways your revelation is lifted up in the world. We pray for our sisters and brothers in Christ, praying as we do today, in house churches in China, in Black storefronts in urban America, on Indian reservations in rural areas, in Black townships in South Africa, in indigenous churches in Africa, in base communities in the barrios of Latin America, in Europe among the foreign workers, in our own communities among the infirm, the homeless, and the dying. Wherever the church is found on the frontiers of mission and service, may your ministry be strengthened and our vision of ministry be stretched. Lord, in your mercy,

For this assembly: May we be enriched by our diversity and dedicated to preparing leadership for the future, acknowledging our present gifts, and remembering those who in the past birthed us into faith. Lord, in your mercy,

For the young Marys and Josephs in our society, and for newborn children, especially those undernourished and without parental love and care: May all be given a home and an atmosphere of home-making. Lord, in your mercy,

For an end to violence, oppression and injustice: As you lead us, Lord, from darkness to light, make us children of the light. May we join with Mary's song that we may be among those who exalt the lowly and fill the hungry with good things, routing out the proud of heart and drawing courage from the power of your arm. Lord, in your mercy,

For our own spirit: With Mary may our hearts be magnified, made much bigger than we imagine them to be. May the new breath of Advent stir in us such ardor that we extend ourselves much more than we thought possible. May we like Mary set out across the barren country without fear, to visit the Elizabeths in our lives. Lord, in your mercy,

[Here other intercessions may be offered.]

Lord, we gather up the prayers of this household, confident that as each day you transform darkness into light you know our deepest thoughts and will refresh our spirits. We pray in the name of the one who transforms principalities and powers and renews heaven and earth, Christ our Lord.

CHRISTMAS MASS AT MIDNIGHT C
CHRISTMAS I C
THE NATIVITY OF OUR LORD 1 C

Sisters and brothers, rejoicing in the love of God that has taken flesh among us in Christ Jesus, let us confidently bring to the Lord the petitions of our heart this Christmas night, saying: Lord, hear our prayer.

For the believing community throughout the world, especially those in positions of leadership, that they might always work to give glory to God and to bring peace to our earth, let us pray to the Lord.

For the church gathered in this place, that we might always bear the good news of God's living presence in our world, towards deepening of Christmas faith and living that faith in love, let us pray to the Lord.

For those lost in the darkness of prejudice, hostility, and fear; for those burdened by the yoke of injustice, terrorism, hunger, and war; and for all our brothers and sisters in any need [especially N.], that the light and life that is the Lord might touch their hearts this night, let us pray to the Lord.

For the homeless, and for the children born in the midst of poverty and pain, that there be room at the inn for all God's people, let us pray to the Lord.

For the sick and the dying among us [especially N.], and for those who care for them, that the God whose love extends from the wood of the manger to the wood of the cross might bless them this night with the gift of peace, let us pray to the Lord.

[Here other intercessions may be offered.]

All loving and gracious God, we thank you for gracing us with the gift of your Son. Confident of your continuing love for us, we have placed our needs before you. Hear and answer our prayers, through that same Christ, newly born this night, our Lord and Savior, forever and ever.

CHRISTMAS MASS DURING THE DAY C
CHRISTMAS III C
THE NATIVITY OF OUR LORD 2 C

Sisters and brothers, confident in the word made flesh and dwelling among us, let us bring to our loving God the petitions in our hearts this Christmas Day, saying: Lord, hear our prayer.

For the community of believers throughout the world, especially those in positions of leadership and authority, that they might direct us toward the service of God's glory and the spread of God's light to the ends of the earth, let us pray to the Lord.

For the church gathered here this Christmas Day, that our worship of the word made flesh might take on flesh in our living the gospel message, let us pray to the Lord.

For all refugees, and for the victims of war, violence, and injustice, that they might know the power of the newborn Savior, let us pray to the Lord.

For all our sisters and brothers in any need [especially N.], let us pray to the Lord.

For all who dwell in the darkness of ignorance and disease, of poverty and homelessness, of division and hate, that the light of Christ might work its wonders this day and this season, let us pray to the Lord.

For the sick and the dying among us, [especially for N.,] for all God's own who are suffering, and for those who care for them, that each might behold the salvation of our God and be blessed by the Prince of Peace, let us pray to the Lord.

[Here other intercessions may be offered.]

All loving and gracious God, we thank you for taking flesh among us in the Lord Jesus Christ. Trusting in a power beyond ourselves, trusting in your enduring love, we have offered our petitions. May you hear and answer them in that same Love, who is Jesus, your Son and our Lord, this Christmas Day and forever.

HOLY FAMILY C
FIRST SUNDAY AFTER CHRISTMAS C

All things have been clothed in grace by the incarnation of our Lord Jesus Christ; all the earth has been enlightened in his dawning. Trusting in the light and grace, let us pray for all people in need and for all the world, saying: Merciful God, hear our prayer.

For the churches, that united in life they may be faithful in witness to your Son come among us, merciful God,

For the poor of the earth, for the victims of warfare [and for the people of N.], that their mourning may be turned into joy, merciful God,

For all families, that they may be renewed in joy, receive the word of mercy into their hearts, and become places of hospitality to the stranger, merciful God,

For the leaders of nations, that they may turn from ways of fear and warfare to the ways of your wisdom and grace, merciful God,

For [our bishop N. and for] all bishops, that they may rejoice in your mercy and faithfully teach the greatness of your coming among us, merciful God,

For this assembly, for our sick, [especially N.,] and for ourselves, that we may be renewed by the light and grace of your incarnate word, merciful God,

[Here other intercessions may be offered.]

Rejoicing in the company of Mary, mother of our Lord, and of all the witnesses of the incarnation, we commend these prayers and all our life to you, O God, through Jesus Christ our Lord.

SECOND SUNDAY AFTER CHRISTMAS C

In the birth of Jesus Christ among the poor of the earth, God has promised to comfort all peoples and to give gladness in exchange for sorrow. Assured by this promise, let us pray for all the earth and all its peoples, saying: Merciful God, hear our prayer.

For the homeless and the hungry, that they may find refuge, merciful God,

For the blind and all the physically disadvantaged, that they may find courage and acceptance, merciful God,

For the cities of the earth, that they may be places of wisdom and justice, merciful God,

For national leaders, courts, and legislatures, that they may protect the weak and serve in humility, merciful God,

For an end to war, merciful God,

For the holy church of God, that it may be made one, merciful God,

For missionaries in all lands, that they may act in courage and love, merciful God,

For this assembly, that we may treasure in our hearts the word spoken in our midst, merciful God,

For the sick [and especially for N.], for those we name before you in our hearts, and for those who will die this day, merciful God,

[Here other intercessions may be offered.]

Joining in thanksgiving with Mary the mother of God, with all those who heard and touched the coming of the word among us, with all angels, and with all the people of God, we commend these prayers and all this longing world to you, O God, through your Son, Jesus Christ our Lord.

THE EPIPHANY OF OUR LORD C

Today we celebrate the manifestation of God's love to all nations, both Jew and Gentile. With confidence let us bring our petitions to God's altar, saying: Lord, hear our prayer.

For God's people throughout the world, especially for those in positions of leadership and authority, that they might spread the good news of God's indiscriminate love, let us pray to the Lord.

For each other, the people of God gathered in this place, that we might always proclaim with our lives the praise of the Lord and so be channels of the call to God's promise and plan, let us pray to the Lord.

For our Jewish brothers and sisters and all who glory in the star of David, that together we might see in the star of Bethlehem not a symbol of division but a call to reconciliation, let us pray to the Lord.

For all victims of prejudice and discrimination, be it based on color, nationality, sex, or creed, that the light of Christ might shine as a beacon in the world's darkness; and for gifts of healing and unity, let us pray to the Lord.

For our brothers and sisters in need; for the poor, the homeless, the hungry, and the abandoned; for the sick and the dying, [especially N.,] that they might find hope and courage in the open arms of the Savior, let us pray to the Lord.

[Here other intercessions may be offered.]

Loving God, we offer you our prayers, some in words, others written in our hearts. Read our hearts; hear our prayers; and continue to shed on us your light, Christ Jesus, who is Lord, this day and forever.

BAPTISM OF OUR LORD C
FIRST SUNDAY AFTER EPIPHANY C

We look in faith today toward the Lord, the one on whom God's favor rests. In confidence, let us bring our petitions to the Lord's altar, saying: Lord, hear our prayer.

For those who lead the believing community throughout the world, that they might lead us on the path of faithful discipleship, let us pray to the Lord.

For the baptized gathered in this church, that we might follow in the path of John the Baptizer and always acknowledge Jesus as Lord, let us pray to the Lord.

For all those preparing for baptism and for their families, and for our newest members, that they might draw closer to the servant who is God's chosen, the light of the nations, and our light, let us pray to the Lord.

For the healing of all those who are blind to God's impartial love; for reconciliation among nations, races, creeds, and all that can divide us; for the gifts of unity and peace, let us pray to the Lord.

For the consolation and support of all who are imprisoned, physically, spiritually, emotionally; for all who are ill [especially N.]; especially for those dying of incurable diseases and those who care for them, let us pray to the Lord.

[Here other intercessions may be offered.]

All loving and ever-faithful God, we thank you for the gift of your Son. As his disciples, we have offered our prayers. Hear them and answer them in his name, Jesus your beloved Son and our beloved Lord, this day and forever.

SECOND SUNDAY IN ORDINARY TIME C
SECOND SUNDAY AFTER EPIPHANY C

As God's chosen and priestly people, let us pray for the needs of the church and the world, saying: O gracious Lord, hear our prayer.

We pray for the people of God, loved wholly by God and sent to be light in the world. O gracious Lord,

For leaders of nations, and for those who serve us in governments, that all people may work for peace and justice, O gracious Lord,

For all who are persecuted, shunned, neglected, or rejected because of prejudice, that they may find welcoming love in our community of faith, O gracious Lord,

For all married couples and their families, that they may share the joy and love of God for all, O gracious Lord,

For all members of our community, that we may recognize the gifts we have received from the Spirit and use them freely for the good of all, O gracious Lord,

For all members of the church community, including the sick, the dying, the deceased, and those who mourn [especially N.], O gracious Lord,

[Here other intercessions may be offered.]

Holy God, lover of the human family and helper of all in need, hear the prayers we offer in faith, and strengthen us in your love. We ask this through Christ our Lord.

THIRD SUNDAY IN ORDINARY TIME C
THIRD SUNDAY AFTER EPIPHANY C

We have heard God's word in faith. Let us now respond in prayer for all the world, saying: Lord, hear our prayer.

For Christian people around the world, that we may become one as Christ wills us to be, let us pray to the Lord.

For all who hear and read God's word with faith, that the Spirit may touch their hearts with joy, let us pray to the Lord.

For all members of the body of Christ, that we may use the gifts God has given us to build up the kingdom of peace and love, let us pray to the Lord.

For ourselves, that we may heed the Spirit's call to help all in suffering or affliction and to bring the good news of God's love to all, let us pray to the Lord.

For the sick and the dying, and those who minister to them; for the deceased and those who mourn them; for all in crisis or need; [and especially for N.,] let us pray to the Lord.

[Here other intercessions may be offered.]

Loving God, we come as your beloved children, presenting the needs and concerns of our hearts. Listen to our prayers, and lead us in your pathways, for we come to you through Christ our Lord.

FOURTH SUNDAY IN ORDINARY TIME C
FOURTH SUNDAY AFTER EPIPHANY C

We are the beloved children of God. In faith and love we come to pray for the church and for the world, saying: Lord, hear our prayer.

For peace on earth and in the hearts of national leaders, we pray to the Lord.

For all the people on earth, that they may listen to the prophets God sends, we pray to the Lord.

For all who teach God's word, that they may be faithful in guiding people to the light of truth and life, we pray to the Lord.

For parents, teachers, and youth workers, that they may live with the gospel each day, sharing their love with all, we pray to the Lord.

For the young people in our community, that they may be inspired by the ideals of Jesus and follow him in their daily living, we pray to the Lord.

For all who are afflicted with pain, sorrow, or loneliness, [especially N.,] and for all who care for them, we pray to the Lord.

[Here other intercessions may be offered.]

God of all nations, look with love on this world and on its people. Bless the work of your creation, and help us to be strong in following Jesus, who is our brother and our Lord, now and forever.

FIFTH SUNDAY IN ORDINARY TIME C
FIFTH SUNDAY AFTER EPIPHANY C

Taught by God's word we pray for the church and the world, saying: Lord, have mercy.

For peace in all lands and in the hearts of all people, we pray:

For all who are Christians, that they may be strong in their love and faith and may work together for greater unity, we pray:

For those preparing for ministry and for all who guide them, that they may be teachers of God's light and love, we pray:

For all members of our civic community, that we may live together with justice and understanding, we pray:

For the sick and the dying [and especially for N.], and for the dead and the bereaved, we pray:

[Here other intercessions may be offered.]

God of wisdom and love, hear the prayers of your beloved children in this community of faith. Bring your help to all in need, granting our prayer through Christ our Lord.

SIXTH SUNDAY IN ORDINARY TIME C
SIXTH SUNDAY AFTER EPIPHANY C
PROPER 1 C

With all our heart and our mind let us offer to God our prayers, saying: Lord, in your mercy, hear our prayer.

Blessed are you, O Lord our God. In Jesus you have made the cursed shrub of desolation to be our tree of life. Cut us away from trust in ourselves, and water our parched and withered hearts with the streams of your love. Lord, in your mercy,

O God, you brought life out of death through the Red Sea waters and through the death and resurrection of our Lord. Call all the peoples of the world out of futile living and believing, that we all may hope in your dominion of justice and peace. Lord, in your mercy,

Holy One, in Jesus you touched the troubled and unclean. Reach out and touch all who are troubled [especially N.]. Heal our diseases. [Look on especially N.] Remove the evil spirit of racism. Let your power cleanse us that we may sing praises to you alone. Lord, in your mercy,

Gracious Lord, your mercy encompasses all creation. Stretch out your gracious hand even as we deny and distort your presence in our midst. Fill us with the hunger which makes us dependent on you alone. May our lives extend your healing hand to all the world. Lord, in your mercy,

Lord, from creation to covenant and from prophets to present day, you have judged those who seek consolation in their possessions. Bless us with the poverty which opens us to your dominion. Call us away from a life which hoards and squanders your creation. Lord, in your mercy,

Abba God, you came to us little and vulnerable. Make us see and become one with the poor that we may share in your dominion. Make us see and become one with the hungry that we may find our satisfaction in serving others. Lord, in your mercy,

[Here other intercessions may be offered.]

Give us, O God, tears of sorrow for this world. May our laughter
grow out of trust that you are indeed Lord of heaven and earth. May
we leap for joy in you, through Christ our Lord.

SEVENTH SUNDAY IN ORDINARY TIME C
SEVENTH SUNDAY AFTER EPIPHANY C
PROPER 2 C

That we may see God's presence in the lives of even the enemy, let us
offer to God the needs of the whole world, saying: Lord, in your mercy,
hear our prayer.

Living God, you spoke to your people of old. Give to your
church ears to hear your voice speaking in our day, even
through those we name as enemy. Lord, in your mercy,

Lord, for the nations of the world we pray. Let not anger consume us. Take away from us false virtue, and break down all
dividing walls of hostility. Lord, in your mercy,

Lord, in Jesus you called us to sacrificial love. Enable us to
serve all those in need, the poor, the homeless, the sick, and
the dying. [Especially we pray for N.] Lord, in your mercy,

Lord, through the hardships of the Hebrew leaders you preserved the life of your people. Comfort all those in distress.
Make of human suffering a gracious gift of life for others. Lord,
in your mercy,

Lord, in Jesus you have given us the first fruit of your dominion. Plant your life-giving Spirit in us and in our land, that we
may bring forth justice and peace. Lord, in your mercy,

[Here other intercessions may be offered.]

Lord, who formed humanity of the dust of the earth, reform us into the
likeness of your Christ. May your mercy pour into our laps. May we
see ourselves as one with those we accuse and so know the joy of
forgiveness given and received, through Christ our Lord.

EIGHTH SUNDAY IN ORDINARY TIME C
EIGHTH SUNDAY AFTER EPIPHANY C
PROPER 3 C

Let us offer to God our prayers for us and for all the world, saying: Lord, in your mercy, hear our prayer.

Almighty God, in ancient days you saved the weak and brought to nothing the oppressor. Frustrate those who work for evil. May we be your arms to aid the orphan and the alien. Lord, in your mercy,

O Lord, you know the interior of our hearts. Confront us with all false allegiances to flag and country, family and friends, religion and tradition. Open our eyes and our ears that we may hear and see your way in our world. Lord, in your mercy,

Lord, you send us prophets, preachers and reformers. Open us to your words, that we may hear and do them. Lord, in your mercy,

Holy God, you called Israel to justice and faithfulness. Bring forth from all your baptized people an abundance of good, a rich harvest of living fruit. Lord, in your mercy,

Gracious Lord, in Jesus you have known the sting of death. Comfort all who mourn. Give joy to all who sorrow. Give courage to all who suffer. Embrace with your arms of mercy all the sick [especially N.]. Look with compassion on all who suffer unjustly. Lord, in your mercy,

[Here other intercessions may be offered.]

Hear our prayers, O Lord, and grant us our desires. Look on all this weary world for the sake of your Son, Jesus Christ our Lord.

LAST SUNDAY AFTER EPIPHANY C
TRANSFIGURATION OF OUR LORD C

Formed by the word and promise of God, let us pray that the merciful glory of God, manifest in all the earth, may drive away all darkness and that God's providence lead all people from death into life, saying: Lord, in your mercy, hear our prayer.

For the church of Christ, that knowing now only in part it may wait in humility and joy to see your full light, Lord, in your mercy,

For preachers, that they may speak clearly of your Christ, transfiguring the words of ancient prophets, Lord, in your mercy,

For catechumens and for us all as we begin to keep Lent, that your word may transfigure our lives, Lord, in your mercy,

For the sick, [for N.,] for the dying, and for all who have asked for our prayers, that you will cause light to shine out of their darkness, Lord, in your mercy,

For the nations of the earth and for their leaders, that they may learn the ways of your peace, Lord, in your mercy,

For all those who seek you, not knowing your name, that they will find that your everlasting mercy has enlightened them and called them by name, Lord, in your mercy,

[Here other intercessions may be offered.]

Before you, O God, are all our prayers and all our needs. You are our life and light, our mercy and hope and our ever-dawning day. Hear us through your Son, Jesus Christ our Lord.

On this day of fasting and prayer, let us offer our prayers to God, pleading for the life God alone can give, and saying: Lord, have mercy.

We pray for the church, all those in the city of Zion, that returning to the Lord we may keep a holy Lent. That all may have life, let us pray to the Lord.

We pray for this assembly of believers, that before we ask God's blessings we gladly receive God's word. That all may have life, let us pray to the Lord.

We pray for all who are preparing for baptism, that they may come to live in God's forgiveness. That all may have life, let us pray to the Lord.

We pray for the nations of the world, that those in authority will hear the call of God to live in peace and righteousness. That all may have life, let us pray to the Lord.

We pray for all in need of home and food, protection and companionship. We pray for all who suffer from war and for all who live in prison and refugee camps. That all may have life, let us pray to the Lord.

We pray for the sick, the suffering, the infirm, the severely handicapped, those are who institutionalized, those who today will die. [We pray especially for N.] That all may have life, let us pray to the Lord.

[Here other intercessions may be offered.]

We remember all those who have followed the call of God [especially N.]. May we live out our time of wilderness wandering and come with them to the joys of heaven.

Gather us all this Lent, O Lord our God, in your embrace, that we may be formed into your likeness of your Son, Jesus Christ our Lord.

FIRST SUNDAY IN LENT C

In this holy season let us turn to God in prayer, saying: Lord, hear our prayer.

For the catechumens and for all the holy people of God [*silence*], that we may be led by the Spirit to hunger for the word of life, let us pray to the Lord.

For the peoples and nations of the world, and for those in authority [*silence*], that power and glory may not turn us from the way of justice and peace, let us pray to the Lord.

For all who are afflicted and oppressed, [especially N.,] that God will open our ears to their cry, let us pray to the Lord.

For this community [*silence*], that we may believe in our hearts and confess with our lips the word that is near, let us pray to the Lord.

For our own needs and those of others [*silence*], that God may be gracious to us in our need, let us pray to the Lord.

[Here other intercessions may be offered.]

Strong and faithful God, hear us as we cry to you. Stretch out your hand to save us, that we may praise you for your mercy. We ask this through Christ our Lord.

SECOND SUNDAY IN LENT C

In this holy season let us turn to God in prayer, saying: Lord, have mercy.

For the catechumens and for all the holy people of God [*silence*], that we may heed the voice of the Lord and reform our ways and our deeds, let us pray to the Lord.

For the peoples and leaders of nations [*silence*], that we may preserve and care for the blessings of this world, let us pray to the Lord

For outcasts and those without home or land [*silence*], that a place of refuge, shelter, and belonging will be theirs, let us pray to the Lord.

For this community [*silence*], that God may grant us the grace to lift our minds above the things of earth and to stand firm in the Lord, let us pray to the Lord.

For our own needs and those of others [especially N.], that we may find shelter and protection under God's wings, let us pray to the Lord.

[Here other intercessions may be offered.]

Come to our aid, Lord God, and grant, by your grace, that we may walk in the footsteps of the crucified Lord and so come with him to the glory you have promised. We ask this through Christ our Lord.

THIRD SUNDAY IN LENT C

In this holy season let us turn to God in prayer, saying: Lord, hear our prayer.

For the catechumens and for all the holy people of God [*silence*], that we may heed the God who calls us to repentance in the events of our lives, let us pray to the Lord.

For this nation and all the nations of the world [*silence*], that we may live in harmony and peace, let us pray to the Lord.

For those enslaved in body or in spirit [*silence*], that God may come to rescue them and grant them freedom, let us pray to the Lord.

For this community [*silence*], that during this holy season God's grace may produce in us the fruit God seeks, let us pray to the Lord.

For our own needs and those of others [especially N.], that
God will not allow us to be tested beyond our strength, let us
pray to the Lord.

[Here other intercessions may be offered.]

*God, ever faithful and true, from of old you have revealed yourself as
one who will be with your people to save them. Be with us in our times
of need, now and always. We ask this through Christ our Lord.*

FOURTH SUNDAY IN LENT C

*In this holy season let us turn to God in prayer, saying: Lord, have
mercy.*

For the catechumens and for all the holy people of God [*silence*], that we may embrace the folly of the cross and become
ministers of reconciliation in a broken world, let us pray to the
Lord.

For this nation and all nations [*silence*], that we may generously
share the produce of the land, both in plenty and in want, let
us pray to the Lord.

For the alienated and rejected of this world [*silence*], that all
may come to know God's welcome to sit down at table, let us
pray to the Lord.

For this community [*silence*], that we may learn from God to
seek the lost and to rejoice when they are found, let us pray to
the Lord.

For our own needs and those of others [especially N.], that
God may be our hope and consolation, let us pray to the Lord.

[Here other intercessions may be offered.]

*God of mercy and compassion, bring us back to you when we stray,
and give us again the joy of proclaiming among the nations your
saving deeds. We ask this through Christ our Lord*

FIFTH SUNDAY IN LENT C

As God's new people, formed in Christ Jesus, let us join in prayer to God who makes all things new, saying: O God our Savior, hear our prayer.

Draw your church more deeply into the reality of Christ's sufferings, so that every one whom you have called in him may show forth the power of his resurrection. O God our Savior,

Renew the spirit of hope in every human society and nation. Invigorate us, that we may strain forward to the future you promise. O God our Savior,

Show your mercy to those who are held back by infidelity to your plans, and free them to receive your word of life. O God our Savior,

Rescue from fear those who are deprived of their human needs or their human rights. Give them their share of the dignity you confer on all your children. O God our Savior,

Grant to this assembly a heart open to your word, that we may embrace your promise, heed your commands, and declare your praise. O God our Savior,

[Here other intercessions may be offered.]

God our Savior and Redeemer, you are constantly at work, bringing forth new things in your creation. Hear the prayers we make to you, and continue to perform ever greater wonders for the entire family of humankind, through your Son, Christ our Lord.

SUNDAY OF THE PASSION C
PALM SUNDAY C

Christ Jesus was obedient unto death on a cross, and exalted by God he continues to plead for all humankind. Let us join him in prayer for all our brothers and sisters, saying: Father, we place our lives in your hands: Lord, hear our prayer.

Establish peace and friendship among all earth's peoples; let violence and enmity give way to concord. Father, we place our lives in your hands:

Renew your church's longing for your reign of justice; may Christians work together to establish what is right in your eyes. Father, we place our lives in your hands:

Grant a share in Christ's exaltation to all who share his degradation, especially to those whose poverty and helplessness are exploited by the powerful. Father, we place our lives in your hands:

Heal the wounds which crime has inflicted on our cities, and help our judges and lawmakers to fashion a society based on trust and respect. Father, we place our lives in your hands:

Open our eyes to the sins we have committed; may our repentance lead us to seek forgiveness, and restore us to the Paradise of your presence. Father, we place our lives in your hands:

[Here other intercessions may be offered.]

Father, the prayer of Christ brought forgiveness to those who crucified him, and the prayer of the thief brought him a place with Christ at your side. Hear the prayers we now make to you, and sustain your people in their need. We make our prayer through Christ, our crucified Lord.

HOLY THURSDAY C
MAUNDY THURSDAY C

*On this night, the Lord Jesus was handed over to sinners. Let us pray
to his Father on behalf of all for whom he died, saying: God, who
washed us in the blood of your Son, have mercy upon us.*

Clarify your church's insight into your presence in the world,
and enable every human being to see in our fellowship the sign
of your new covenant. God, who washed us in the blood of
your Son,

Teach our national and local leaders the power of humility, and
enable them to work selflessly for the good of all. God, who
washed us in the blood of your Son,

Reconcile the divided Christians churches, and grant peace to
nations and religious groups hostile to one another. God, who
washed us in the blood of your Son,

Come to the aid of the earth's starving peoples, and give them
their rightful share of the food you lavish on all your creatures.
God, who washed us in the blood of your Son,

Heal the bodies of the wounded and diseased [especially N.].
Heal the hearts of those betrayed by their loved ones. God,
who washed us in the blood of your Son,

Forgive the sins of this people which calls on you; let the bread
we break and the cup we drink save us from evil and free us to
obey your word. God, who washed us in the blood of your
Son,

[Here other intercessions may be offered.]

*God our Savior, hear the prayers of your family, gathered to proclaim
the death of your Son until he comes. Pour forth on all humankind
your blessings of life, harmony, and true freedom, through Christ our
Lord.*

EASTER VIGIL C

Christ died for our sins and rose for our justification. Being at peace with God, let us pray with confidence, saying: Through the blood of your Son, save us, O God.

Let the wind of your Spirit move within your church; remove from it all that does not obey your creating word. Through the blood of your Son,

Keep free from sin those who have been joined to Christ's death through baptism, and let their new life bring fresh enthusiasm to every Christian. Through the blood of your Son,

Show your glory by liberating all who are oppressed; banish economic and political exploitation from the world. Through the blood of your Son,

Protect young people from the danger of drugs and materialism; teach them to seek what is good, that they may grow to the full stature of Christ. Through the blood of your Son,

Uphold by your power those suffering from incurable and stigmatizing diseases; join their sufferings to Christ's passion, that they may share his glory. Through the blood of your Son,

Strengthen this community in Christ's self-giving love; give us the grace to live no longer for ourselves but for him who died and rose for us. Through the blood of your Son,

[Here other intercessions may be offered.]

Eternal God, you are the strength and courage of all who call upon you. Hear our prayers, and stretch forth your mighty arm to save and protect all our brothers and sisters in the human family, through the gracious power of Jesus Christ, our risen Lord.

EASTER DAY C
THE RESURRECTION OF OUR LORD C

Christ is risen! He is risen indeed! At this the heavenly choirs of
angels rejoice, the earth exults, and mother church is glad. Therefore I
ask you, who praise the loving-kindness of almighty God, to join in
prayer for all of God's people, and for all people everywhere according
to their needs. That all may know the benefits of the paschal victory of
Christ, we pray, saying: Lord, in your mercy, hear our prayer.

Almighty and merciful God, we give you thanks for those who
have come through the waters of rebirth into the promised land
of your eternal kingdom. Guide all your baptized people who
struggle to know and to do your will in the kingdoms of this
world, that by their lives they may show forth the new life in
Christ to all nations. Lord, in your mercy,

We give you thanks for those who struggle for peace and justice in the world. Guide their efforts, that they may act with
prudence and vision to plant the signs of your dominion in the
earth. Lord, in your mercy,

We give you thanks that Mary Magdalene found healing in the
encounter with the risen Christ. Give wholeness and peace to
all those in need: the sick [especially N.], the unloved and the
forgotten, the poor and the hungry, the dying and the bereaved [especially N.]. Lord, in your mercy,

We give you thanks for the abiding presence of your Son in
word and sacrament. As we feast this Easter Day on the true
bread from heaven, set our minds on things above, that we
may gain a new perspective on the things that are on earth.
Lord, in your mercy,

[Here other intercessions may be offered.]

We give you thanks for those who have gone before us in the
faith, who now rest from their labors awaiting the resurrection
to eternal life [especially N.]. May we, like them, remain faithful to the end and share in the fruits of the victory of Christ,
the paschal lamb who takes away the sin of the world. Lord, in
your mercy,

Hear our prayers on behalf of those for whom we pray, and give us peace in this time of our paschal rejoicing, for the sake of your Son, Jesus Christ, our risen and exalted Lord.

SECOND SUNDAY OF EASTER C

In this Eastertide we celebrate and proclaim the signs of Jesus, that all might believe that he is the Christ, the Son of God, and that believing they may have life in his name. Therefore, that everyone may experience the new life in Christ in the midst of the old life of sin and doubt, let us pray for all God's people, and for all people everywhere according to their needs, saying: Lord, have mercy.

That amid all the doubts which threaten to destroy the community of faith, Christ's peace may be shared and experienced for the strengthening of belief, let us pray to the Lord.

That all who have come to new birth in holy baptism and all who have received the forgiveness of sins in absolution may live in peace with each other, let us pray to the Lord.

That the sick, the infirm, and the disturbed [especially N.] might experience the healing power of the Spirit of the risen Christ, let us pray to the Lord.

That those who participate in the eucharistic meal may taste and see the feast to come in the presence of the one who died and is alive forevermore, let us pray to the Lord.

[Here other intercessions may be offered.]

That all who have died in the faith [especially N.] may serve as examples to us who continue in our pilgrimage on earth, let us pray to the Lord.

Lord, we believe. Help our unbelief, and hear us for the sake of the one who died for our sins and rose again for our justification, even Jesus Christ, the first and the last, the living one, in whose name we pray.

THIRD SUNDAY OF EASTER C

In this Eastertide the hosts of heaven proclaim, "Worthy is the Lamb who was slain, to receive power and wealth and wisdom and might and honor and glory and blessing." Therefore I invite you, who join the worship of the Lamb with the angels and archangels and all the company of heaven, to pray for all for whom he died, saying: Lord, in your mercy, hear our prayer.

Almighty and merciful God, you exalted your Son as Leader and Savior, and raised him above all rule and authority. Give your faithful people courage to follow him in obedience to you wherever we are called to witness. Lord, in your mercy,

As the disciples of Jesus ventured out at his word, so give us the faith to trust and obey his word in our lives as we pursue together the mission of the church. Lord, in your mercy,

As the disciples of Jesus shared food with their Master, so give us the generosity to share what we have with those in need. Lord, in your mercy,

As Jesus commanded Peter to feed his sheep, so strengthen all the clergy to preach the gospel and administer the sacraments with faithfulness and conviction. Lord, in your mercy,

As the disciples shared a meal with the risen Lord, so by your Holy Spirit bring us in faith to the table of the Lord where we may feast on him who is our priest and victim. Lord, in your mercy,

[Here other intercessions may be offered.]

Bring us at last with all the saints [especially N.] to the adoration of the Lamb who was slain. Lord, in your mercy,

To the one who sits upon the throne and to the Lamb be blessing and honor and glory and might forever and ever.

FOURTH SUNDAY OF EASTER C

In this Eastertide we rejoice together at the resurrection of Christ. That the world may be commended to the care of the Good Shepherd, let us pray for the whole people of God in Christ Jesus, and for all people according to their needs, saying: Lord, hear our prayer.

For preachers of the word [especially N. our bishop and N. our clergy], that they may follow in the tradition of Paul and Barnabas, speaking out boldly to the edification of all people, let us pray to the Lord.

For Christian churches throughout the world, that they may experience unity and may follow Christ their Shepherd, let us pray to the Lord.

For the nations of the world, that they may turn from oppression, imperialism, and warfare, and seek only the welfare of their peoples, let us pray to the Lord.

For the homeless, the hungry, and the sick [especially N.], that they may find comfort in the one who shelters them with holy presence, guides them to springs of living water, and wipes away every tear from their eyes, let us pray to the Lord.

For all mothers and those who give motherly care, that they may follow the example of the Good Shepherd who leads his children to good pasture, let us pray to the Lord.

[Here other intercessions may be offered.]

In thanksgiving for the holy apostles Barnabas and Paul, all the saints and martyrs [and especially N.], let us give praise to the Lord.

Into your hands, O Lord, we commend all for whom we pray, trusting in your mercy, through Jesus Christ our Lord.

FIFTH SUNDAY OF EASTER C

Gathered together in the name and power of our risen Lord, through whom the glory of God is revealed, let us offer our prayers to almighty God, saying: Lord, hear our prayer.

That heavenly peace may descend upon us and upon the whole world, we pray to you, O Lord.

That we may love one another as Christ has commanded us, we pray to you, O Lord.

That the church throughout the world and in this congregation may be united in peace, empowered by the Spirit, and faithful in its mission to all humankind, we pray to you, O Lord.

That the power of Christ's victory over death may show itself among us, bringing freedom, joy, light, and life to those in need [especially N.], we pray to you, O Lord.

[Here other intercessions may be offered.]

Together with all others united to us in the communion of the risen Lord [especially N.], for all that we need in this life and in your eternal dominion, we pray to you, O Lord.

Grant, eternal God, that we who are made one with Jesus Christ in the power of his death and resurrection may show forth in our lives the love which proclaims us his disciples, that the world may believe in you and be saved, through Christ our Lord.

SIXTH SUNDAY OF EASTER C

Let us pray in union with our risen Lord, in the power of the Holy Spirit, the Counselor, saying: Lord, have mercy.

For the peace of Christ, his own gift to his apostles, let us pray to the Lord.

For all who hold authority in this world [especially N.] and in the church [especially N.], that the Holy Spirit may guide them into the ways of justice, peace, and truth, for the good of all people everywhere, let us pray to the Lord.

For those whose hearts are troubled, through hunger, fear, poverty, sickness, loneliness, or for whatever reason [especially N.], that the love of Christ may make its home with them and fill them with all peace, let us pray to the Lord.

For all who have been baptized into Christ's death and resurrection, that we may love Christ and keep his word, and be made one with each other with Christ in God, let us pray to the Lord.

For the whole creation, men, women, children, plants, animals, and the wonders of the universe, that we may all in our varied ways give praise to the God who made and loves us, let us pray to the Lord.

For those who till the earth and those who fish in the waters to bring food to the world, and for all whose hand is open to give bread to the hungry, that all may enjoy the fruits of the earth, let us pray to the Lord.

[Here other intercessions may be offered.]

Lord Jesus Christ, you have sent your Holy Spirit to teach us and to bring to remembrance all you have done in the power of God. Be known to us, as you have promised. Hear our prayers, grant us your peace and love, and give us those things which we need in this life. You live and reign for ever and ever.

ASCENSION DAY C

Our risen and ascended Lord offers up priestly intercessions for us before the throne of heavenly grace. Let us offer our prayers through our Lord, saying: O Christ, hear us.

That your sovereign rule may lead the nations of this world into the ways of justice and peace,

That until you return in glory your church may fulfill your commission to proclaim the gospel to all people everywhere,

That your Holy Spirit may guide us and lead us into all truth,

That your love may bind us to one another in the communion of the Holy Spirit,

Remember in their needs, O Lord, your brothers and sisters who are sick, hungry, imprisoned, unjustly treated or abused [especially N.]. That you will sent them your heavenly aid,

[Here other intercessions may be offered.]

Ascended Lord, you have not left us, but gone before us into the heavenly glory. Raise these our prayers to heaven, and present them to God in union with your eternal sacrifice, that we may know your divine love in this life and may be one with you in your Godhead in the life to come.

SEVENTH SUNDAY OF EASTER C

As Jesus Christ offered his great high priestly prayer for us who have come to belief through the ministry of his apostolic church, let us pray with Christ and in his name for the church, the world, and all people everywhere, saying: Lord, have mercy.

For the peace of the world, that all humanity may live in freedom with justice and dignity, let us pray to the Lord.

For the unity of the church in Christ Jesus, that we may be one in Christ as Christ is one with God, let us pray to the Lord.

For the apostolic mission of the church, that we may bring all humanity to the knowledge and love of God in Christ, let us pray to the Lord.

For the deaconal ministry of the church, that we may serve one another in Christ's name, let us pray to the Lord.

For all who need the love and power of Christ [especially N.], let us pray to the Lord.

[Here other intercessions may be offered.]

For all the saints in glory [especially N.], and all those whom we have known and loved who though dead are alive in Christ [especially N.], let us pray to the Lord.

O God our Lord, Jesus Christ, our great high priest, lives to make intercession for us. Hear the prayers of your church assembled in his name and presence. Show your glory in all the world that it may believe in you and be saved, through Christ our Lord.

PENTECOST SUNDAY C
DAY OF PENTECOST C

On this Pentecost Sunday, let us raise our prayer to God for the Spirit sent to anoint us, saying: Lord, hear our prayer.

For the spirit of joy in the church, that our Eastertide Alleluia resound throughout the year, we pray to the Lord.

For the spirit of peace in the world, that all peoples, especially nations in conflict, may live in harmony, we pray to the Lord.

For the spirit of justice for the needy, that victims of prejudice, exploitation, and crime be set free, we pray to the Lord.

For the spirit of unity in our assembly, that our weakness make us strong and our differences made us rich, we pray to the Lord.

For the spirit of hope in the future, that we and all who have died may drink of the fruit of the vine in glory, we pray to the Lord.

[Here other intercessions may be offered.]

Good and gracious God, send forth your Spirit into our hearts. Wipe away the fear between churches, nations, and families. Tear down the walls that divide us, and make us one through Christ our Lord.

TRINITY SUNDAY C

On this Trinity Sunday, let us lift our petitions to the Father, the Son, and the Holy Spirit, saying: Lord, hear our prayer.

For the ministers of the church, that they build a community of love which flows from the community of God, we pray to the Lord.

For every member of the human family, that we be guided to all truth by the Spirit of truth, we pray to the Lord.

For the stewards of the earth, that they accept creation as a wondrous gift and work to preserve its beauty, we pray to the Lord.

For the sick [especially N.], that their affliction lead to endurance, their endurance to virtue, and their virtue to hope, we pray to the Lord.

For us who celebrate community here, that our labors spread joy and our witness bring peace, we pray to the Lord.

[Here other intercessions may be offered.]

O God, our Father from whom good things flow, we thank you and praise you, singing Holy. Answer our prayer and bring us hope through Christ your Son, who celebrates life with you in the unity of the Spirit, now and forever.

THE BODY AND BLOOD OF CHRIST C

We hunger for the life of God among us and in our world. In the name of our Lord Jesus, let us call upon the one who satisfies every human need, saying: Lord, hear our prayer.

For the church scattered throughout the world, that united in the one bread and one cup of the eucharist a single voice might proclaim in word and deed the saving death of Christ, let us pray to the Lord.

For the nations of the world and for their leaders, that an equal sharing of the earth's bounty might bring greater peace and joy to all people, let us pray to the Lord.

For those who have no bread, no cup; for the homeless and the abandoned; [especially for N.;] that women and men of good will might respond generously to their need, let us pray to the Lord.

For this community of faith, that strengthened by the eucharist we may be united in a communion of hearts and minds and so offer our lives in loving service to the world, let us pray to the Lord.

[Here other intercessions may be offered.]

Merciful God, the love of Christ poured out for us in his body and blood is the faithful sign of your presence and power in our lives. Hear now the prayers of your faithful people, and out of the abundance of your mercy grant us what we truly need, for we call upon you in the name of Jesus, who is our food and our Lord, forever and ever.

NINTH SUNDAY IN ORDINARY TIME C
PROPER 4 C
SECOND SUNDAY AFTER PENTECOST C

Let us go with the Jewish elders and ask Jesus to save his servants, saying: Lord, in your mercy, hear our prayer.

Save the church, that it become a strong sign of love and hope for others. Lord, in your mercy,

Save the world from nuclear destruction, from the horror of war, from organized crime, and from ignorance. Lord, in your mercy,

Save foreigners: save Russians, Arabs, Israelis, Indians, Australians, Germans, Cubans, [N.,] all the people of the earth, that peace reign in the land. Lord, in your mercy,

Save businesspersons, politicians, doctors, and people of the media, that as they try to win approval they also serve the truth. Lord, in your mercy,

Save us from our lies, that we become a community mirroring goodness in the heart of every man, woman, and child. Lord, in your mercy,

[Here other intercessions may be offered.]

God of all the nations, cure your servants and give us health. Keep us faithful to the gospel of your Son. To you be glory forever.

TENTH SUNDAY IN ORDINARY TIME C
PROPER 5 C
THIRD SUNDAY AFTER PENTECOST C

Like the dead man who sat up, let us rise to speak our prayers from the heart, saying: Lord, hear our prayer.

For the church, that its leaders come fully alive and give hope for all the members, we pray to the Lord.

That people everywhere take courage in approaching death and celebrate life with greater joy, we pray to the Lord.

For Christians, Jews, and Moslems, that we speak more kindly of one another in church, synagogue, and mosque, we pray to the Lord.

For widows, widowers, divorced parents, orphans, and all single people, that they find love in community and comfort in God, we pray to the Lord.

For all in any need [especially N.], we pray to the Lord.

[Here other intercessions may be offered.]

For dying people and for the dead, especially children and loved ones, that they see God face to face, we pray to the Lord.

God of kings, prophets, children, and widows, breathe your spirit of life into the living and the dead. Make us one with you and one another, and let all creation praise your name, now and forever.

ELEVENTH SUNDAY IN ORDINARY TIME C
PROPER 6 C
FOURTH SUNDAY AFTER PENTECOST C

The God who wants us to walk in peace knows that we need to find that peace. We call on this God of forgiveness to listen to our prayers, saying: O gracious God, hear our prayer.

For hearts that will not judge what is sinful in other people, O gracious God,

For minds that will acknowledge injustices to ourselves and oppression in all of its forms, O gracious God,

For feelings that will allow us to respect the religious commitment of Muslims, Jews, and other Christians, as well as the commitment of nonbelievers to the human family, O gracious God,

For wills that are graced with the courage to make visible the presence of Jesus Christ in the church, O gracious God,

For bodies and spirits healed; [especially for N.;] O gracious God,

[Here other intercessions may be offered.]

O Holy One of Israel, God of love and truth, help us to know our own sinfulness and need. Free us from the desire always to be right. Give us the peace of Christ, and carry us forward to care for those in need, through Christ our Lord.

TWELFTH SUNDAY IN ORDINARY TIME C
PROPER 7 C
FIFTH SUNDAY AFTER PENTECOST C

Let us pray that God pour out on us a spirit of grace and petition, as on Jerusalem of old, and hear us as we pray, saying: We stand in need, O God; Lord, have mercy.

That the law of faith which guides us be our standard in judging the laws of land and church and culture, and that our lives be conformed to the faithful love of Christ, we stand in need, O God:

That parishioners weakened through illness of mind or body feel your protective hand and our tangible care, we stand in need, O God:

That we who call Christ messiah be empowered to carry the cross of insult as we work for freedom in the third world, we stand in need, O God:

That the paths we walk be wide enough for all peoples, for the homeless, for aliens in flight, for prisoners, for persons of all colors, for all who are ostracized, for those dying of incurable disease, for all who in Christ you call your own, we stand in need, O God:

[Here other intercessions may be offered.]

God, our mother and father, deepen our trust in you. Watch over us day and night, and protect us from harm's way. Let us guard one another, that none may be excluded from our circle, embraced in Jesus Christ our Lord.

THIRTEENTH SUNDAY IN ORDINARY TIME C
PROPER 8 C
SIXTH SUNDAY AFTER PENTECOST C

The God who yearns for us calls us to come as a people. Let us not turn away, but rather go to this God with our needs, saying: Forget us not, O holy One, hear our prayer.

For all the leaders and the followers in the church, that we know when to give up the unimportant things, forget us not, O holy One:

For people in this community in the grip of addiction, and for all who need release from what enslaves, forget us not, O holy One:

For patience with those who incite to war, and for the wisdom to move into the reign of God's unending peace, forget us not, O holy One:

For the fearless ones who uphold human rights in every land of oppression [especially N.], and for all who live where liberty is held hostage in the name of law and order, forget us not, O holy One:

For all who suffer [especially N.], forget us not, O holy One:

For this assembly, as we serve the sisters and brothers among us and as we work outside church doors, forget us not, O holy One:

[Here other intercessions may be offered.]

God of light and life, strip us of selfishness and the loneliness it brings. Help us to accept the gift of mutual love, with its shared pleasures and pain. Tear down all our fences that we can run to you as one family, one people, through Christ our Lord.

FOURTEENTH SUNDAY IN ORDINARY TIME C
PROPER 9 C
SEVENTH SUNDAY AFTER PENTECOST C

God, the mother who nurtures us, is also God of power without end. We call on this God of comfort and might, saying: O mighty and gracious God, hear our prayer.

For your church, that the good news we spread always heed the physical and social needs of our listeners, O mighty and gracious God,

For leaders of nations, that they bring peace to their lands, destroying the demons of poverty and inequity, O mighty and gracious God,

For the dying among us, that they be granted dignity and seren ity as they await the comforting arms of their mothering God, O mighty and gracious God,

For people of all ages nearing breakdown, that they glimpse Jerusalem's hope, and that their hearts rejoice again, O mighty and gracious God,

[Here other intercessions may be offered.]

God of glory and tenderness, engrave in us the images of your sacred stories. Relieve us of our many burdens, and let our lives give honest testimony to your dominion, through Christ our Lord.

FIFTEENTH SUNDAY IN ORDINARY TIME C
PROPER 10 C
EIGHTH SUNDAY AFTER PENTECOST C

Many people's needs press upon our daily lives and fill our daily news. That we may respond as neighbors, let us ask the Lord for help, saying: Lord, in your mercy, hear our prayer.

Help us to be neighbors to strangers, to people of every land and tongue and culture. Lord, in your mercy,

Help us to be neighbors to all who suffer, the lonely, the sick and the sorrowing [especially N.]. Lord, in your mercy,

Help us to be neighbors to people of every creed, to Christians and Muslims, Jews and Hindus, Buddhists and atheists. Lord, in your mercy,

Help us to be neighbors to the enemy, the alien, the despised, those with whom we disagree. Lord, in your mercy,

Help us to be neighbors to everyone we pass on the road, to salespeople, co-workers, family, and passers-by. Lord, in your mercy,

Help us to be neighbors to one another, and thus to share our lives as we share your word and your supper. Lord, in your mercy,

[Here other intercessions may be offered.]

Lord God, you formed us in love; you command us to live in your love. Hear the prayers we make in the name of the Son you sent to dwell among us, the neighbor who is attentive to all our needs, Jesus Christ our Lord.

SIXTEENTH SUNDAY IN ORDINARY TIME C
PROPER 11 C
NINTH SUNDAY AFTER PENTECOST C

Like Martha, we have much to do; like Mary, we listen to the Lord's voice. From the complexity of our lives, let us raise our voices in prayer, saying: Lord, hear our prayer.

Over the thunder of war, we hear the Lord's call to peace, and we pray for wise leadership.

Amid the quarrels which divide the church, we hear the Lord's call to unity, and we pray for reconciliation.

Above the barrage of commercials, we hear the Lord's call to generosity, and we pray for the poor.

Through the bustle of our daily lives, we hear the Lord's call to love, and we pray for patience with one another.

In the cries of the suffering, we hear the Lord's call to compassion, and we pray for the sick and the suffering [especially N.]

In the songs we raise together, we hear the Lord's call to each of us, and we pray for one another.

[Here other intercessions may be offered.]

Father of Jesus, hear our prayers. Hear in them the voice of your Son, your word of love to us. We listen for his voice as we pray in his name: Jesus Christ, Lord of heaven and earth forever.

SEVENTEENTH SUNDAY IN ORDINARY TIME C
PROPER 12 C
TENTH SUNDAY AFTER PENTECOST C

With the Lord's encouraging words still sounding in our ears, let us frame again the prayers which linger in all human hearts, saying: Hear us, O Lord.

We are weary of war and threats of war. Let us pray for peace in our world, saying,

We fear for our children. Let us pray for all children, their health and well-being, saying,

We are anxious about our security. Let us pray for an end to hunger and want, saying,

We yearn for faith in an uncertain world. Let us pray for all who preach the gospel, saying,

We tremble at our own vulnerability. Let us pray for the victims of illness, accident, and disaster, [especially N.,] saying,

We carry worry in our hearts. Let us pray for the needs we can hardly bear to name, saying,

[Here other intercessions may be offered.]

Loving God, our Father, you fashioned the human heart; you know the needs that make it ache. Hear us, your children, praying as your Son taught us. His is the name we invoke; his is the kingdom we await: Jesus Christ, the Lord.

EIGHTEENTH SUNDAY IN ORDINARY TIME C
PROPER 13 C
ELEVENTH SUNDAY AFTER PENTECOST C

Let us pray together for the riches that endure, saying: Lord, have mercy.

For faith enough to proclaim God's word, let us pray to the Lord.

For compassion enough to comfort the suffering, let us pray to the Lord.

For hope enough to bolster the discouraged, let us pray to the Lord.

For courage enough to tackle the problems of nations and races, let us pray to the Lord.

For forgiveness enough to heal old wounds, let us pray to the Lord.

For love enough to bind us to all in Christ's community, let us pray to the Lord.

[Here other intercessions may be offered.]

Giver of all gifts, what we are and what we have come from you. Enrich us with your blessings; impoverish us in the service of the Son who lived and died in poverty. He is our greatest wealth, Jesus Christ, our Savior and our Lord.

NINETEENTH SUNDAY IN ORDINARY TIME C
PROPER 14 C
TWELFTH SUNDAY AFTER PENTECOST C

We have been taught to pray by the Lord. So with one voice we ask for us all, saying: Lord, hear our prayer.

To face the promise of life with the courage you give, we pray you, O Lord:

To face the evil of life with the goodness you give, we pray you, O Lord:

To face the death of life with the love you give, we pray you, O Lord:

To face our aged with your unfailing mind, we pray you, O Lord:

To face our young with your unfailing heart, we pray you, O Lord:

To face our poor with your unfailing hand, we pray you, O Lord:

To face all war with loathing, as you do, we pray you, O Lord:

To face all peace with longing, as you do, we pray you, O Lord:

[Here other intercessions may be offered.]

It is your way with life that we want, O Lord, that we ask of you. Ana you have offered it. It is a joy to live by you. May those who do not know this find it out through your presence to their world. We pray in Jesus' name.

TWENTIETH SUNDAY IN ORDINARY TIME C
PROPER 15 C
THIRTEENTH SUNDAY AFTER PENTECOST C

We hope to see the Lord's work in this world, answering God's call and not fighting against it. Let us pray with one voice, saying: Lord, hear our prayer.

Help us to heed and not to harm the messenger of peace, we pray you, O Lord:

Help us to bear and not to break the discipline of truth, we pray you, O Lord:

Help us to feel and never to fear the love of Christ, we pray you, O Lord:

To those who must bear a message of peace, give a Christlike courage, we pray you, O Lord:

To those who must teach the ways of truth, give a Christlike strength, we pray you, O Lord:

To those who must love when hatred rules, give a Christlike heart, we pray you, O Lord:

Take away war; take away lies; take away hatred, we pray you, O Lord:

Send us prophets; send us teachers, sons and daughters of your name, we pray you, O Lord.

[Here other intercessions may be offered.]

O Lord, we have learned what to ask you through your Son, the peacemaker, the teacher of truth, who loved without limit. It is you that he revealed. We want to be like you in him, through whom we pray.

TWENTY-FIRST SUNDAY IN ORDINARY TIME C
PROPER 16 C
FOURTEENTH SUNDAY AFTER PENTECOST C

We would be empty without God's gifts, and we would be selfish if we kept them to ourselves. For God's generosity let us pray, saying: Lord, hear our prayer.

Teach us to love and share your gift of peace, we pray you, O Lord.

Teach us to love and share your gift of mind, we pray you, O Lord.

Teach us to love and share your gift of life, we pray you, O Lord.

Do not leave us to merchants of war, we pray you, O Lord.

Do not leave us to merchants of lies, we pray you, O Lord.

Do not leave us to merchants of death, we pray you, O Lord.

Teach us to cherish all truth that is not ours, we pray you, O Lord.

Teach us to cherish all life that is not ours, we pray you, O Lord.

Hear our prayers for all in need [especially N.], we pray you, O Lord.

[Here other intercessions may be offered.]

You enter our lives, O God, by the gift of yourself. It is the way we are to enter yours. Teach us that generosity. Teach it to everyone alive our brothers and sisters in this world. We pray through Christ, our teacher and brother.

TWENTY-SECOND SUNDAY IN ORDINARY TIME C
PROPER 17 C
FIFTEENTH SUNDAY AFTER PENTECOST C

God has searched for us to teach us how to search for one another. That we may learn to live in God's new Jerusalem, generous with life, let us pray together, saying: Lord, hear our prayer.

You come to us unarmed. May we never use you as a way to war, we pray you, O God.

You come to us penniless. May we never use you as a way to wealth, we pray you, O God.

You come to us innocent. May we never use you as a way to corruption, we pray you, O God.

May we use your peaceful self as a way to make peace, we pray you, O God.

May we use your penniless self as a way to beg for alms, we pray you, O Lord.

May we use your innocent self as a way of curing sin, we pray you, O lord.

Shame us out of arrogance, O Lord, arrogance of power and place, we pray you, O Lord.

Win us with the love you have for the least of things, we pray you, O Lord.

Hear our prayers for all in any need [especially N.]. we pray you, O Lord.

[Here other intercessions may be offered.]

It would be a joy for us to be as you are, O Lord, toward the least of things on earth. We ask for your peacefulness, your humility, your innocence, both for ourselves, and for all the world. For there is no going home to you without our brothers and sisters, and through Christ our Lord.

TWENTY-THIRD SUNDAY IN ORDINARY TIME C
PROPER 18 C
SIXTEENTH SUNDAY AFTER PENTECOST C

We do not know the wisdom of God nor what the Lord intends. But we do know God's mercy. So we confidently gather our needs and present them to God, the Father, saying: Lord, have mercy.

For the leaders of the church, that they may be single-hearted in love of the Lord and in service to the people, we pray to the Lord.

For the imprisoned and the oppressed, the solitary and the unwanted, that they may know the love of Christ in the care of the Christian community, we pray to the Lord.

For those who decide to follow Jesus, that they may keep sight of his cross and the joy it holds for them, we pray to the Lord.

For those who live far from family and friends, that they may find companionship and friendship, we pray to the Lord.

For the young who are searching for their lives, and for those who seek honest work, that they may have the wisdom to know their gifts and use them for the human community, we pray to the Lord.

For all who make decisions of consequence, that they may seek the Lord and choose what will bring life, we pray to the Lord.

For all in any need [especially N.], we pray to the Lord.

[Here other intercessions may be offered.]

Loving Creator, you are our life and our prosperity. We who make mighty plans know that before you they are little. Fill us with your wisdom; hear us and the needs of all the world, that we may care well for your creation. We ask this in the name of Jesus the Lord.

TWENTY-FOURTH SUNDAY IN ORDINARY TIME C
PROPER 19 C
SEVENTEENTH SUNDAY AFTER PENTECOST C

Our God wraps us round in love and embraces us with mercy. There is nothing we need hide. Let us bring our needs and the needs of the whole human family to God's loving care, saying: Lord, hear our prayer.

That the leaders of the church will be, like Moses, one with their people and outspoken on their behalf, we pray to the Lord.

That the church will spend itself in search of the lost of this world, the homeless, the addicted, the uneducated, the ill, the rejected, and that we will welcome them to our household, we pray to the Lord.

That all who are far from home will live in safety, we pray to the Lord.

For all who are alienated from us and who stay away from this table, that they may return home, and that we may be watching to greet them, we pray to the Lord.

For the sick, the aged, the lonely, [especially N.], and any who cannot be with us today, that they may know our kindness and God's mercy, we pray to the Lord.

That peace and forgiveness will mark our lives together as families, we pray to the Lord.

[Here other intercessions may be offered.]

God of promises, you have brought us a long way and have kept us safe in our journey to you. Hear us now, and answer our prayers with delight. Teach us to run to you for all we need. We ask this in the name of Jesus, the Lord.

TWENTY-FIFTH SUNDAY IN ORDINARY TIME C
PROPER 20 C
EIGHTEENTH SUNDAY AFTER PENTECOST C

God is just, God is one. But we are often fragmented and consumed by many wants. Let us gather our needs now and offer them confidently and simply to God, our Father, saying: Lord, hear our prayer.

For the leaders of the world powers, that they may be just and honorable in their dealings with one another, we pray to the Lord.

For peace, a reduction of arms, and an end to war and terrorism, we pray to the Lord.

That the church and its leaders may be ingenious and tireless in preaching the good news, we pray to the Lord.

That all Christians may hold their goods and money lightly and use them for the sake of God's dominion, we pray to the Lord.

That all elected officials may respond to the needs of their community and serve the common good, we pray to the Lord.

That employees and employers may act honestly in their workplaces and treat one another with dignity, we pray to the Lord.

For the poor, the hungry, the homeless, and the jobless, we pray to the Lord.

That the wealthy and those with no material want may use their bounty in keeping with their calling, we pray to the Lord.

[Here other intercessions may be offered.]

Just God, one God, we live in this world and look for the world to come. Teach us what to ask for: give us all we need. Make us life-givers with you who build your dominion here, in the name of Jesus the Lord.

TWENTY-SIXTH SUNDAY IN ORDINARY TIME C
PROPER 21 C
NINETEENTH SUNDAY AFTER PENTECOST C

God alone is our help. We lift up our needs and the needs of the whole human family, saying: Lord, have mercy.

For those who lead the people of God, that they may seek after integrity and be true to their call to service, we pray to the Lord.

For Christians everywhere, that we may be rich in good works and generously share what we have, we pray to the Lord.

That our eyes may be open to see poverty and human need, and that seeing, we may act justly, we pray to the Lord.

For an end to the abyss between rich and poor, in our community, in this nation, and throughout the world, we pray to the Lord.

That our young people may learn to love charity, justice, and a gentle spirit, we pray to the Lord.

For the aged, the infirm, the lonely, the homeless, [especially N.,] and for all who need help to live with dignity, we pray to the Lord.

That those who are imprisoned for the sake of the gospel may bear bold and glad witness to the Lord, we pray to the Lord.

[Here other intercessions may be offered.]

Giver of all life, we ask you to sustain our life and the life of the world. Hear our cries for help. Make us as generous as you are in answering those who turn to you. We ask this in the name of Jesus, the Lord.

TWENTY-SEVENTH SUNDAY IN ORDINARY TIME C
PROPER 22 C
TWENTIETH SUNDAY AFTER PENTECOST C

Let us pray for the whole human family and for the world of which we are a part, saying: Lord, in your mercy, hear our prayer.

O God, you are unresting in movement, serene in the stillness, inspiring zeal while counseling patience, calling us from paths that lead to ease and indifference. That washed anew each day by our baptism, we wait for your coming, not hardening our hearts nor forsaking our faith, but vowing dedication in mind and in will and lifting hearts and hands in holy obedience to your will: Lord, in your mercy,

That leaders of all segments of society, government and military, business and industry, all popular and social endeavor, will reject impotent rhetoric and will speak the truth for the honest edification of the kingdom among us: Lord, in your mercy,

That we together with those in our families and in our communities, those who suffer from illness and disease, loneliness and despair [especially N.], and those we name silently before you, may bask in the warmth and joy and love of the Spirit: Lord, in your mercy,

That those we criticize and scorn will become our brothers and sisters, and that we make the first step toward reconciliation: Lord, in your mercy,

[Here other intercessions may be offered.]

That the memory of our loved ones and of all the saints will keep us steadily on the path to which you point us: Lord, in your mercy,

Hear these words, O Lord, as you hear and understand the unspoken thoughts of our hearts and minds, and grant their fulfillment through Christ our Lord.

TWENTY-EIGHTH SUNDAY IN ORDINARY TIME C
PROPER 23 C
TWENTY-FIRST SUNDAY AFTER PENTECOST C

Let us bow before almighty God, offering our thanksgiving and making known our requests for the whole human family and for all the world, saying: Lord, in your mercy, hear our prayer.

O God of morning and evening, noonday's brightest sun and midnight's darkest hour, hear us as we offer you our praise and dare to sing your new song. For confidence to believe that your gift of life requires our most willing effort, and that accepting that gift we never forget to offer our thanks: Lord, in your mercy,

For the land in which we live, that we see it as your gift, and that all its peoples work together with all our strength to conform it to your holy will: Lord, in your mercy,

For courage and commitment, that we wait upon those in need, and that they may see in us your loving care for them: Lord, in your mercy,

For all in any need, for those in pain and in sorrow, [especially for N.,] that your gift of hope will strengthen them on their way to wholeness: Lord, in your mercy,

[Here other intercessions may be offered.]

For the ties that bind us to those who have gone before, and that with all our loved ones and all the blessed saints we keep in view the joyous feast that is to come: Lord, in your mercy,

Hear these words, O Lord, as you hear and understand the unspoken thoughts of our hearts and minds, and grant their fulfillment through Christ our Lord.

TWENTY-NINTH SUNDAY IN ORDINARY TIME C
PROPER 24 C
TWENTY-SECOND SUNDAY AFTER PENTECOST C

*Confident that in the Son's teaching and through the Spirit's leading
we shall be heard, let us lift hearts and voices to God, saying: Lord, in
your mercy, hear our prayer.*

O God, ever promising deliverance to your people, hold out
your hands to us, and hear our common supplications. For
courage to pray, calling out day and night for all that you have
promised: Lord, in your mercy,

For diligence in reading your word, and for the whole church
as we ponder the inspiration you granted to those who have
gone before us, that we may understand your message to us:
Lord, in your mercy,

For boldness to speak your word humbly to others, for constancy and courage, and for all to whom we speak: Lord, in
your mercy,

For your love in us, that you may use our hands and our hearts
to carry your love to others: Lord, in your mercy,

For your warmth and strength and power for all in any need
[especially N.]: Lord, in your mercy,

[Here other intercessions may be offered.]

For unfailing remembrance of the blessed dead, especially [for
N. and] for those whose names and faces fill our days and
nights, that we may always give thanks for their lives, and that
we live in fervent expectation of joy together with them in your
house forever: Lord, in your mercy,

*Hear these words, O Lord, as you hear and understand the unspoken
thoughts of our hearts and minds, and grant their fulfillment through
Christ our Lord.*

THIRTIETH SUNDAY IN ORDINARY TIME C
PROPER 25 C
TWENTY-THIRD SUNDAY AFTER PENTECOST C

Grateful for our blessings, determined in our mission, expectant for fulfillment, let the church cry out to God, saying: Lord, have mercy.

For faithfulness, that we trust in God's promise and live in confident obedience, let us pray to the Lord.

For openness in reaching out to all the people of the world, that together we may walk out of darkness into God's light, let us pray to the Lord.

For humility, that we glory only in God's forgiving, generous love, let us pray to the Lord.

For perseverance, that we daily seek out all who are hurt and cry and are in need, let us pray to the Lord.

For comfort for all those in any need; for health for the sick and food for the hungry; [for N.;] that touched by God they may shine with the brilliance of God's light, let us pray to the Lord.

[Here other intercessions may be offered.]

Blessed are all those who have fought the good fight and now share in the wondrous vision God promised from the beginning. That we may keep them always in our sight, eager for the day of our joyous reunion, let us pray to the Lord.

O God, you make glad the hearts of all who dwell in your house. Accept our gratitude, enjoy our praise, and save us. Grant the fulfillment of our prayers through Christ our Lord.

THIRTY-FIRST SUNDAY IN ORDINARY TIME C
PROPER 26 C
TWENTY-FOURTH SUNDAY AFTER PENTECOST C

We know our need of God's mercy. That the name of Jesus be glorified, let us commend our lives and all that we have to God's care, saying: Lord, in your mercy, hear our prayer.

O God, you are no discriminator of persons. Look then with love on all those who in this world are disregarded or despised. May all who seek salvation find a home in your heart and in the house of your church. Lord, in your mercy,

O God, lover of all who wander and who seek, you have taken up your dwelling among those who desire life and those who need compassion and understanding. Open their eyes to your presence, as Jesus opened the eyes of Zacchaeus by eating at his table. Lord, in your mercy,

O God, you have given your command that the riches of this world be turned to the service of the needy and the poor Grant that those who control wealth and its distribution may be inspired by a strong sense of compassion and a desire for justice. Lord, in your mercy,

O God, you are the God of the sinner and not of the just. Grant that we may despise none of those to whom you please to give your love. Lord, in your mercy,

O God, may the desire to follow Christ consume our whole being, and make our hearts and homes receptive to your call, with the same zeal with which Zacchaeus sought Jesus and responded to his presence. Lord, in your mercy,

[Here other intercessions may be offered.]

Savior God, as Zacchaeus was blessed to receive Jesus into his home and responded with generosity to this gift, so may we and those whom we have here remembered be blessed in his name, so that it may be glorified without end. We make this prayer in Jesus' name, for he is Lord forever and ever.

THIRTY-SECOND SUNDAY IN ORDINARY TIME C
PROPER 27 C
TWENTY-FIFTH SUNDAY AFTER PENTECOST C

Our God is the God of the living and not of the dead. Even as we dwell in the midst of death, we are heartened by God's promises and turn to God in confident supplication, saying: Lord, hear our prayer.

O God, promised of the living, when your glory appears our joy will be full. That until that day Christian communities may give testimony in word and deed that they are children of the resurrection, we pray to our God.

That those who suffer affliction and loss [especially N.] may find their lives transformed in the hope of a new age, we pray to our God.

That the persecuted and those who suffer injustice and contempt may be protected by God's grace from the evil of persons and systems, we pray to our God.

That those who have suffered pain in their marriages and those who live with separated parents may find God's peace and promise in the heart of the church, we pray to our God.

That in its response to Christ's word, the church may bring obedience to the Spirit and concern for the troubled to its consideration of the ethical questions of our times, we pray to our God.

[Here other intercessions may be offered.]

That the dead may rest in God's bosom, with Sarah and Abraham, with Moses and Miriam, and with all who have died in the hope of the resurrection, we pray to our God.

O God, promised of the ages, in the midst of all anxieties and fears we ask you to hear us, as we make supplication for those whose lives need hope, until that day when your glory appears and our joy will be full. We make our prayer in the name of Jesus, who lives with you and the Holy Spirit, forever and ever.

THIRTY-THIRD SUNDAY IN ORDINARY TIME C
PROPER 28 C
TWENTY-SIXTH SUNDAY AFTER PENTECOST C

Knowing that a mother does not desert her children, let us turn to God, asking God to embrace with lovingkindness all those whose lives are troubled and afflicted by human evil. Let us beg God not to delay, saying: Lord, hear our prayer.

God of Jesus Christ, even in our own day many are handed over to injustice and persecution, and many suffer want and hunger; come to rule the earth with justice, and delay not in sending your transforming love.

God of Jesus Christ, even in our own day many families are torn apart by internal strife, sisters and brothers reach out to one another with hating hands, peoples and nations are divided by anger: delay not with your peace.

God of Jesus Christ, even in our own day children are not spared, but are apprenticed to hatred, rejected by their own parents, forbidden even life itself: delay not with your motherly affection.

God of Jesus Christ, even in our own day the followers of your child of promise are separated by prejudice and bitter division: delay not in making us into one people.

God of Jesus Christ, even in our own day many find contempt and rejection within your church: delay not in bringing the harmony of love to your chosen.

[Here other intercessions may be offered.]

O compassionate God, in Jesus, your child of promise, we know and await the life and peace of which you have assured us. We look forward in longing, hoping for ourselves and for those whom we have remembered, in the name of the same child who lives with you in the communion of the Holy Spirit, forever and ever.

TWENTY-SEVENTH SUNDAY AFTER PENTECOST C

Let us pray for the whole people of God in Christ Jesus and for all people according to their needs, saying: Lord, in your mercy, hear our prayer.

For peoples who are captive, oppressed, and despised [especially N.], that you will be present with them, speaking your name in comfort and in power, Lord, in your mercy,

For the cities of the earth, for Calcutta, Jakarta, Beijing, Capetown, Rome, [N.,] and New York, that you will be present in them, speaking your name in comfort and in power, Lord, in your mercy,

For the sick among us, [for N.,] for those whom we name in our hearts before you, that you will be present to them, speaking your name in comfort and in power, Lord, in your mercy,

For those in authority among us, for all stewards of your many gifts, that you will be present to them, speaking your name in comfort and in power, Lord, in your mercy,

For all the church of God, and for this assembly gathered in your presence, that you will be present to us, speaking your name in comfort and in power, Lord, in your mercy,

[Here other intercessions may be offered.]

For those who will die this day, and for the beloved dead whom we have entrusted to you, that you will be present to them, speaking your name in comfort and in power, Lord, in your mercy,

Blessed God, in the resurrection of Jesus Christ your Son you have destroyed death and comforted the whole earth. Let his reign come soon among us, among all whose lives cry out to you for mercy, among all the people of the earth. For unto you is due all honor and glory, to the Father and the Son and the Holy Spirit, now and forever.

LAST SUNDAY, CHRIST THE KING C
PROPER 29 C
CHRIST THE KING C

*In the life of Jesus Christ in our midst, we have known God's judg-
ment and mercy, and in the glory of Jesus we acclaim the image of God
invisible. With the whole church we turn to Christ this day, acknowledging that he alone rules in truth, as we say: When you come to rule,
remember us, O Lord.*

Jesus, Savior and Judge, you have confounded earthly judgment by choosing to be numbered among the transgressors.
May your words comfort all who are in prison, all judged guilty
by society or church, and all who live on the margins of the
human family. When you come to rule,

Jesus, condemned and powerless before your enemies, grant to
the leaders of peoples to know that their rule is in the service of
a greater law. When you come to rule,

Christ, first-born of the dead, through the blood of your cross
you give unity to the divided. Give to the church the hope of
resurrection; may we recognize the image of God in your own
rising. When you come to rule,

Christ, image of the invisible God, free us from holding you in
images of our own making. Grant that in the Spirit we may see
all power and all life transformed by the compassion of the
cross. When you come to rule,

[Here other intercessions may be offered.]

Jesus, pelican feeding your young with your own blood, may
the dead who have partaken of your chalice be with you in
paradise. When you come to rule,

204 *Last Sunday in Ordinary Time, Christ the King C*
Proper 29 C
Christ the King, Last Sunday after Pentecost C

We acclaim you, Jesus Christ, as the judge condemned to judgment, knowing that in your death the world is judged. Grant that the world may seek God's justice rather than human wisdom, and that all victims of human cruelty may share in the victory of life revealed to us in your death and rising. We join our prayers with the pleading of your blood poured forth at God's right hand, where you rule in the Spirit forever and ever.

Last Sunday in Ordinary Time, Christ the King C **205**
Proper 29 C
Christ the King, Last Sunday after Pentecost C

HOLY DAYS

JANUARY 1
MARY, MOTHER OF GOD
HOLY NAME
NAME OF JESUS

The good news of incarnation shows dramatically God's love for a fallen world. Let us pray to the God of wonder, saying: Lord, hear our prayer.

For the church, those who bear the name Christian here and throughout the world, let us pray to the Lord.

For God's blessing of peace upon all nations and upon all who dwell therein, let us pray to the Lord.

For those who rejoice during this holiday season: friends, relatives, and neighbors, generous givers and gracious receivers, let us pray to the Lord.

For those who mourn during this holiday season, the grief-stricken and the despondent, the lonely and the forgotten, [especially N.,] let us pray to the Lord.

For all whom winter treats harshly, those without home or shelter, those without heating or clothing, let us pray to the Lord.

[Here other intercessions may be offered.]

For those who have gone before us, family, friends, and neighbors, mighty saints and repentant sinners, let us pray to the Lord.

As shepherds were astonished by your marvels, O God, so too do we stand in awe of your goodness. Be merciful to us today in our need that we may learn to be your compassion in our world. We ask this through Christ the Lord.

FEBRUARY 2
THE PRESENTATION OF OUR LORD

Made like us in every respect, our high priest knows our suffering and intercedes for us before the throne of mercy. Let us pray through Christ, saying: Lord, have mercy.

For our church, that it be a light to all nations and a beacon for all peoples, let us pray to the Lord.

For God's people Israel, first to hear the word of God, let us pray to the Lord.

For enlightened minds and hearts among those who act and work for the public good, let us pray to the Lord.

For God's reign of peace, that no people need live in the fear of death, let us pray to the Lord.

For those who speak and those who hear the prophetic word today, let us pray to the Lord.

For wisdom in old age and for fidelity in youth, let us pray to the Lord.

For those who suffer from winter's cold, let us pray to the Lord.

For all who walk in darkness, facing illness, death, and misfortune [especially N.], let us pray to the Lord.

[Here other intercessions may be offered.]

God of mercy, be our light in times of darkness and our comfort in times of affliction. May we be as light in a darkened world, proclaiming your faithful love. We ask this through Christ, our one high priest, who lives and reigns with you and the Spirit, one God, forever and ever.

MARCH 25
THE ANNUNCIATION OF OUR LORD

Let us pray with Christ, with Mary and with the church, interceding for the grace to do God's will, saying: Lord, hear our prayer.

That the church, like its Lord, may learn to submit gladly to the will of God, and may faithfully live according to God's word, let us pray for grace from the Lord.

That the church may find its unity in the will and mission of its Lord, let us pray for grace from the Lord.

That the leaders of the nations may serve justice, follow the path of peace, and so respond to the incarnate God, let us pray for grace from the Lord.

That the needy, the poor, and those who live on the margins of society may be comforted as they await justice, and that we may serve their needs, let us pray for grace from the Lord.

That the sick, the suffering, the dying, and all who mourn may come to know the power of God, and that we may offer them [especially N.] to your will and care, let us pray for grace from the Lord.

That this assembly may be filled with the Holy Spirit, may rejoice in the sacrifice of ourselves in God's service, and with blessed Mary may delight in obedience to God's will done in us, let us pray for grace from the Lord.

[Here other intercessions may be offered.]

Lord, God, in the virgin's womb with wondrous art you have made a holy dwelling in the flesh. Come according to the ancient promise, O Immanuel, and show yourself to be God with us, that we may offer the praise worthy of so great a love and may receive eternal salvation through Jesus Christ our Lord.

MAY 31
THE VISITATION

The Holy One of Israel, God of might and God of tenderness, is in our midst. Let us pray to our God, saying: Lord, hear our prayer.

For our church--
    its members,
    its mission,
    its ministry--
let us pray to the Lord.

For the lowly--
    society's forgotten ones,
    society's neglected ones,
    society's unwanted ones--
let us pray to the Lord.

For the hungry--
    those starving for food and drink,
    those craving attentive care,
    those thirsting for justice--
let us pray to the Lord.

For the persecuted--
    imprisoned for beliefs,
    oppressed by poverty,
    victimized by war and strife--
let us pray to the Lord.

For care and healing--
    for the brokenhearted,
    for the despairing,
    for the terrorized--
let us pray to the Lord.

[Here other intercessions may be offered.]

Compassionate God, you are in our midst, the Holy One of Israel. May we love and labor together so that one day all may rejoice in your saving mercy, through Christ our Lord.

AUGUST 6
THE TRANSFIGURATION

With our eyes fixed on Christ, the beloved Son who intercedes for us, let us offer our prayer with confident faith before the throne of God, saying: Lord, have mercy.

That the church of Christ may be ever attentive to his voice, persevering in prayer and zealous in his service, let us pray to the Lord.

That Christ, the morning star, may dawn upon the hearts of all and herald a new day of justice and peace, let us pray to the Lord.

That those whose lives are overshadowed by physical pain or anguish of spirit [especially N.] may know the healing touch of Christ and the transfiguring power of his resurrection, let us pray to the Lord.

That we who have been called by Christ to this mountain of prayer may find strength here to be his witnesses in the world, let us pray to the Lord.

[Here other intercessions may be offered.]

That those who during their earthly pilgrimage acknowledged the dominion of Christ [especially N.] and all whose faith is known to God alone may be drawn into the radiant joy of heaven's kingdom and behold the face of God, let us pray to the Lord.

God of majesty and power, whose beloved Son is your word of truth and the light shining in our darkness, receive the prayers of your church, and grant that all peoples may come to know the peace of your kingdom and the splendor of your name. We ask this through Christ our Lord.

AUGUST 15
ASSUMPTION OF THE BLESSED VIRGIN MARY
ST. MARY THE VIRGIN
MARY, THE MOTHER OF OUR LORD

God our Savior works revolutions in the earth and turns the world upside down. Let us proclaim the greatness of the Lord and rejoice in our God, praying to the holy and mighty one, saying: Lord, have mercy.

For the God-fearing, that God look with favor on them from generation to generation, let us pray to the Lord.

For justice in all the earth, that with a mighty arm God scatter the proud, cast down the haughty, and lift up the lowly, let us pray to the Lord.

For the hungry, that they may be fed, let us pray to the Lord.

For those who hunger after righteousness, that they may be filled with good things, let us pray to the Lord.

For the just distribution of the wealth of the world, that none go hungry while others are surfeited, let us pray to the Lord.

For the Jews, the descendents of Abraham, that they be faithful to their ancient covenant with God and that we with them inherit the promises of God, let us pray to the Lord.

[Here other intercessions may be offered.]

For all the people of God, that with blessed Mary, the virgin mother of our Lord, and with all the saints, we rejoice as children and heirs of God, redeemed by Christ her son, let us pray to the Lord.

The salvation and the power and the kingdom of our God and the authority of his Christ have come. We proclaim the greatness of the Lord, and we rejoice in God our Savior, praising God in his Son our Lord, now and forever.

Assumption of the Blessed Virgin Mary **213**
St. Mary the Virgin
Mary, the Mother of Our Lord

SEPTEMBER 29
MICHAEL, GABRIEL, AND RAPHAEL
ST. MICHAEL AND ALL ANGELS

Drawing near to the throne of the living God, and to countless angels in festal gathering, with Jesus as our Mediator in whose blood we are washed clean, let us offer our prayer, saying: Lord, hear our prayer.

For the universal church, that protected by the archangel Michael it may boldly proclaim that God alone is Sovereign and there is no other, let us pray to the Lord.

For our world scarred by violence and war, that attentive to the glad tidings announced by the archangel Gabriel all peoples may see in Christ the sure way to justice and peace, let us pray to the Lord.

For those in any anguish of body, mind, or spirit [especially N.], that accompanied by the prayers of the archangel Raphael and receiving comfort from many brothers and sisters they may find healing and hope on their pilgrimage to God, let us pray to the Lord.

For this eucharistic assembly, that our worship may be acceptable in the sight of God and our witness courageous in the midst of the world, let us pray to the Lord.

[Here other intercessions may be offered.]

For those who have died in Christ [especially N.] and for all the departed, that choirs of angels may accompany them to the blessed vision of peace in the eternal Jerusalem on high, let us pray to the Lord.

In the presence of the angels, O Lord, we sing your praise. Receive the prayers we offer, and answer as may be best for us, and as you know us and love us in Christ Jesus our Lord.

NOVEMBER 1
ALL SAINTS

Cleansed in the blood of the Lamb, and one in communion with all the saints of every time and place, let us offer our prayers to the God who loves us, saying: Lord, hear our prayer.

For the holy church of God throughout the world, that the Lord may confirm it in faith, sustain it in hope, and deepen its communion in charity, let us pray to the Lord.

For those who wield earthly power, that they may recognize in the disciples of Jesus children of God anxious to serve in building up the earthly city, let us pray to the Lord.

For those beset by persecution for righteousness' sake and those weighed down by trial and distress, that the example of the saints may give them courage and the help of believers give them hope, let us pray to the Lord.

For this assembly gathered to celebrate the eucharist in communion with the church in heaven and throughout the world, that nourished by the word of truth and the bread of life we may bear witness in our own generation to the timeless gospel of Christ, let us pray to the Lord.

[Here other intercessions may be offered.]

For those who departed this life in faith and in the fear of God [especially N.], that they may join the innumerable throng of holy ones gathered before the throne and the Lamb, let us pray to the Lord.

Holy God, mighty God, immortal God, adored by angels and praised by the saints, receive the prayers of your holy church, and grant them in accordance with your gracious will, through Christ our Lord.

FOR THE UNITY OF ALL CHRISTIANS
FOR THE UNITY OF THE CHURCH
UNITY

Brothers and sisters in the faith, from the nations of the earth God has called forth one people to be the sign of the unity intended for all humankind. Let us offer our prayers for the church and for its mission in the world, saying: Lord, hear our prayer.

For the people of the earth, that where there is strife and division, the gift of peace may be the reward of all who work for justice, let us pray to the Lord.

For the church of Jesus Christ, that where there is weakness health may be restored, and where there is division unity may be nourished, let us pray to the Lord.

For all leaders in the church, that where there is jealousy or distrust, a spirit of forgiveness and compassion may nurture humble service, let us pray to the Lord.

For all who are called to preach the gospel, that in the presence of fear and anxiety the message of hope may be proclaimed courageously and effectively, let us pray to the Lord.

For all missionaries in foreign lands, that when faced with hardship and testing, they may be strengthened in their mission by the Spirit of God, let us pray to the Lord.

For our community and our families, that where there is misunderstanding or discord, we may receive the grace to forgive and so rejoice in the peace of Christ, let us pray to the Lord.

[Here other intercessions may be offered.]

God of unity and peace, in baptism you have made us one people in the body of your Son. Hear us, as with one voice we offer you these prayers in the name of Jesus, who is Lord forever and ever.

216 *For the Unity of All Christians*
For the Unity of the Church
Unity